The Screen Arts

A GUIDE TO FILM AND
TELEVISION APPRECIATION

The SCREEN ARTS

A GUIDE TO FILM AND TELEVISION APPRECIATION

by Edward Fischer

 A SEARCH BOOK : SHEED AND WARD : NEW YORK

© SHEED & WARD, INC., 1960

LIBRARY OF CONGRESS CARD NUMBER 60-12869

A SEARCH BOOK
published by Sheed and Ward, New York, 1969

MANUFACTURED IN THE UNITED STATES OF AMERICA

TO MARY

Grateful acknowledgment is made to the editors of *Ave Maria, America* and *The Critic* for their kind permission to reprint material which first appeared in their pages.

Contents

The Author To
The Reader

Too often I hear the lean mice of trivialities nibbling at my allotted chunk of time. When I gather with strangers in a poorly illuminated vastness to watch a motion picture or sit with my family at home to watch a television program, the question keeps intruding, "Is it worth the time?" For I am more concerned with getting my time's worth than my money's worth.

When it comes to using mass communications the question is one of how much time can you afford rather than how much money can you afford. A quite humble income buys the newspaper, several magazines, a handful of motion picture tickets, a television set and a radio. You get your money's worth even though you use the newspaper only to wrap garbage, save the magazines for the Boy Scout paper drive, go to the movies to enjoy the conditioned air and keep the TV set and radio in case there is an alert you ought to be in on.

In mass communications the time problem might, in fact, be the biggest moral problem of all. When the word *morality* is mentioned in the same sentence with the words *motion pictures* and *television* it usually has something to do with a complaint about low-cut necklines or violence, a complaint that puts the blame on the industry. But the audience ought to share some blame. Anyone who slumps there hour after hour watching inane shimmerings on a screen is guilty of wanton time killing. Everyone has a more noble destiny than that.

I am not against recreation and relaxation. Anyone doing what he is supposed to be doing needs to recharge the batteries from time to time, but this recharging should take place at a certain altitude. Recreation ought to expand the spirit a fraction of an inch, or at least not shrink it. Anyone who sops up movies and television programs without discrimination is getting more than his share of the shoddy, the phony, the tinny, and his spirit will be narrowed and coarsened by the experience.

WHY BOTHER?

It is possible to use films and TV, not to kill time, but to live beyond what our own living can be. For one thing, these can be used, like literature, to give some feeling for the texture of life. Of course only the best films and television programs do that. Let us look at some definite examples.

Paddy Chayefsky's play, *Marty,* first on television and then on film, has in it the texture of life. It is about Marty Pilletti, a butcher, whose soul is as lonely as a freight train's whistle. He lives in the Bronx and hangs around with a bunch of fellows whose lives are hemmed in by mean circumstance and small imagination. Marty is fat and homely and thirty-four. His mother and the women who come to his butcher shop chide him for not getting married; they keep stinging him with, "You ought to be ashamed of yourself, Marty, a man your age and not married." He wants to get married, but nobody will have him. By chance he meets Clara, a plain Jane, a "dog" in the language of the neighborhood. She too has passed beyond lonesomeness on down into loneliness.

The story of Marty's and Clara's aching need for each other helps the audience live beyond its own living. The story gives insight and understanding, and, inevitably, compassion with the problem of loneliness. *Marty* is as saturated with the theme of loneliness as *Macbeth* is saturated with the theme of ambition.

Thornton Wilder's *The Skin of Our Teeth* does a remarkable job of making the audience *feel* man's fallen nature. It is something of a morality play that was written for the stage and later became a teledrama.

The Antrobus family represents every man who ever lived or who ever will live. Through it the audience gets insights into the flaws of human nature and realizes how man continually fails because he never really learns from other people's mistakes. The play is full of man's monotonous struggle against his weaknesses and against the forces of nature, but it is not pessimistic. Optimism prevails because man insists on keeping alive Religion, symbolized by the Bible, and Learning, symbolized by Homer, Archimedes and Aristotle.

Another Wilder play that has the texture of life is *Our Town*. It was written for the stage and later brought to motion picture and television audiences.

As an example of what I mean by the texture of life, or teaching a truth of life, take the scene where Emily, the newly buried young mother, is permitted to leave the cemetery and return to Grover's Corners for one day. She is told it must be a quite ordinary day and she chooses her twelfth birthday. We see her in the kitchen at daybreak watching her mother get breakfast. In the scene Emily is, at once, a child of twelve and a mature woman who can look back on life with the eyes of one who has departed it. When she speaks as the child, her mother hears her, but when she speaks as the woman returned from the grave only the audience and the Stage Manager can hear. It goes something like this:

Emily says softly, more in wonder than in grief, "I can't bear it. They're so young and beautiful. Why did they have to get old? I can't look at everything hard enough. . . . Oh, Mama, just look at me one minute as though you really saw

me. . . . It goes so fast. We don't have time to look at one
another."

She breaks down and sobs to the Stage Manager: "I didn't
realize. So all this was going on and we never noticed. Take
me back—up the hill—to my grave. But first: Wait! One more
look. Goodbye, goodbye world. Goodbye, Grover's Corners.
. . . Mama and Papa. . . . Goodbye to clock's ticking. . . . and
Mama's sunflowers. And food and coffee. And new-ironed
dresses and hot baths. . . . and sleeping and waking up. Oh,
earth you're too wonderful for anyone to realize you."

She asks abruptly, "Does any human being ever realize life
while they live it?—every, every minute?"

"No," says the Stage Manager. "The saints and poets maybe
—they do some."

"I'm ready to go back," says Emily.

These three plays—*Marty, The Skin of Our Teeth* and
Our Town—are examples of recreation at its best. They truly
refresh. They lift the spirit and seem to sharpen the senses—
they are humanizing experiences. They make us "see" more,
and understand more, and feel more deeply. As Emily would
say, they make us "realize" life, if only momentarily.

Films and television plays with the texture of life in them
are not the only ones worth attending to. Television offers
useful, informational programs, such as the documentaries
on *Twentieth Century* and *Conquest* and the conversations on
Small World. The films offer such entertainments as *Lili, The
Mouse That Roared* and *The Green Man*, entertainments that
have substance to them. They are not "great art," but they are
not tinny. They do not send you from the theater feeling the
whole world is flat and stale. They do not stultify the spirit.

This stultification of the spirit is also a moral problem.
Father Gerald Vann, O.P., in writing about the movies in
The Commonweal, said, "We are so accustomed to living in
a world of man-made ugliness that it may never occur to us
that ugliness of that sort means degradation, and degradation

is a moral evil. It may never occur to us that the wanton creation of ugliness is a sin as the wanton infliction of pain is a sin."

Father Vann thinks that the great moral problem in motion pictures might be "the degradation of the human spirit through the aesthetically squalid." There's the rub—the aesthetically squalid. Some people are alert to double-meaning quips on television shows and to over-exposure in foreign films and yet are not pained by the aesthetically squalid. So long as he is cagey about double meanings and over-exposure, a producer can keep these people placated while he goes to and fro in the land uglying-up God's world with the phony and the tinny. If the producer plays his clichés right he may even get an award from groups that would be shocked to hear that they are promoting things which degrade the human spirit.

Aesthetic squalor is not new to our time, but it has taken on a new seriousness with the rise of mass communications, especially with the growth of television. As John Shanley, radio-television editor of the New York *Times* said, "If we were to imagine the components of culture in the United States as a group of buildings in a community, the structure representing television would be the biggest in town." He believes that television has a greater influence on American culture than does the motion picture, the stage, the art gallery, the concert hall or the book.

When the truth of the power of television dawned on one college professor, he said, "It's as dangerous to culture as the atom bomb is to civilization." The professor, and all of us who teach, might be especially careful about looking down on any means of communication; our own inadequacies are only too clear. Had we developed discernment in the classroom, there would be better TV programs, better motion pictures and better everything in the field of mass communications. Schools have done a better job in teaching facts and figures than they have in teaching discernment.

To be definite about this problem, one has only to remember one of the nights television hit one of its highest and one of its lowest levels all in the same ninety minutes. While *The Green Pastures* was singing over one network, Mike Todd's Madison Square Garden party was cluttering up another. The critics sang as a chorus their praises of *The Green Pastures,* but according to the polls the critics seemed to be the only ones watching it; everyone else was tuned to Mike Todd's party. As Walt Whitman said, "To have great poets there must be a great audience," and this can be reworded to read, "To have television with some soul there must be audiences with enough soul to appreciate it."

THE PURPOSE OF THIS BOOK

Developing appreciation is a touchy business. A man might readily admit that he cannot drive a nail, or make a speech, or write a letter, but it is a rare soul who willingly admits he does not know what is good in motion pictures and television. As a friend of mine who is a newspaper editor says, "Everybody thinks he can do three things better than anybody else in the world—handle a drunk, put out a fire and run a newspaper," and to this he might add, "criticize motion pictures and television."

Most people have as standards only their likes and dislikes. They walk out of a movie saying, "It was good, I liked it," or "It was no good, I didn't like it." The whole world of the arts revolves around whether or not they like something. It never dawns on them that a critic might sometimes say, "It was good, but I didn't like it," or "It was no good, but I liked it."

I have used the word *standards* in the previous paragraph with an uneasy spirit. *Standards* sounds so scientific, like *The Bureau of Standards,* as though a work of art could be put on a scale and weighed, or held against a ruler and measured. There *are* standards for motion pictures and for television;

many are explained in the pages which follow, and there is even a list in the back of the book, but they cannot be used like a tire-pressure gauge or a mechanic's check list. An artist cannot keep a list of standards at his elbow to make sure his work is distinguished in every detail, nor can a critic cold-bloodedly hold such a list up to a work of art.

Art is art; it is not bookkeeping.

The artist and the critic both work from sensitized feelings and highly developed intuitions. Reading about standards helps somewhat in sensitizing the feelings and in developing intuitions. But it is also possible to memorize all the standards ever printed and still have vulgar taste. The capacity to enjoy and appreciate is developed by studying standards and by coming into frequent contact with the best things in the arts, especially under the guidance of a cultivated mind. This system eventually leads to attitudes and to habits of mind that are more satisfying to the viewer than a collection of his uncultivated likes and dislikes.

It is the hope of this book that it may lead the reader to a deeper appreciation of the good and the best in movies and television, and thereby make more enjoyable our regular excursions into the wonderful world of the screen arts.

1. Artistic Truth

THE TEXTURE OF LIFE
THE CELLULOID MUSE
PAINLESS PIETY
BELIEVING ONE'S FICTION

ALTHOUGH the screenplay writer, the novelist and the playwright use different techniques, all are alike under the skin because all need be concerned with artistic truth. They are stuck with a common duty: to explain man to himself in the realm of thought and feeling and action.

Through his characters a writer ought to create a bond between himself and his audience. The bond should be one of honest recognition and not one of wishful thinking. If it brings to this meeting something more than just breathing bodies, the audience should know deep in the marrow, until it is almost an ache, that the writer is helping it see the way life is. The audience should feel that here is something of significance which it is sharing with the writer. Those observations of Emily in *Our Town*, quoted a few pages back, are pieces of significance, fragments of immortal truth. To put it the other way around: what the writer shares should not be synthetic illumination or sham sensibility.

A motion picture might be rough-hewn technically and still be a work of art, or it may have a high technical polish—excellent camera work, wonderful lighting and perfect sound—and still be as insubstantial as tinkling brass and sounding cymbals because it lacks artistic truth. Perhaps the best way to explain what I mean by artistic truth is to point to its presence and its absence in some films of recent years: *The Old Man and the Sea* and *The Inn of the Sixth Happiness; Middle of the Night* and *That Kind of Woman.*

THE TEXTURE OF LIFE

In *The Old Man and the Sea,* an old man fishes for marlin. In *The Inn of the Sixth Happiness,* a young woman fishes for souls. The old man's humble pursuit is presented more artistically than is the young woman's noble mission. The old man rings true. The writer knew him to the core, and that is why he can take the audience down below surface emotions. He felt for the old man, and he felt with the old man, and he communicates this emotion to the audience to give the picture what Henry James called "felt life."

The Inn of the Sixth Happiness stays nearer to surface emotions. The audience never really knows the young woman, never really knows why she does what she does, and so she is not as believable as the old man. This film has all the craftsmanship of a good *Saturday Evening Post* story. It can be admired as a professional job of carpentry—it fashions incidents and nails them together well, even better than does *The Old Man*—but it does not rise above excellent carpentry.

As a novel, *The Old Man and the Sea* was not easily adapted to the screen. So much of it deals with the thoughts of an old man, and that presents a production problem, for the camera that can photograph the thoughts of an old man has not yet been invented. The film gets around this by borrowing from documentary technique: it has very little dialogue and a great deal of narration as the events unfold in pantomime on the screen. The narrator seems to be reading directly from the book. As you listen to him you come to realize how much poetry there is in Hemingway's prose, and you realize what poets mean when they say that poetry is something that ought to be heard rather than just seen on a printed page.

Sometimes, in fact, you feel that you could close your eyes and just enjoy the narration. This does not mean that the picture has sacrificed the visual for the sake of sound. The camera work of James Wong Howe, the directing of John Sturgis and the acting of Spencer Tracy are all so expert that if the sound system in the theater broke down the audience could still follow the story from the action on the screen.

The story is simple—few pictures have ever been less complicated. Because the story is so simple, *how* it is told is more important here than in most pictures. It will have to stand or fall on the *how* of it.

An old fisherman in Havana has fished the Gulf for eighty-four days without luck. On the eighty-fifth day he hooks the biggest marlin ever taken in those waters. The contest between the old man and the marlin takes up quite a bit of screen time, and it is to the credit of the actor, the director, the cameraman and the film editor that this does not get boring. Their problem was especially difficult because the editing of the contest has to be in slower, more rhythmic cuts than the slam-bang editing usually found in fight sequences. The slower paced editing is necessary to keep the poetic mood of the picture.

After the old man has the marlin lashed to the side of his boat and starts for Havana the sharks attack. The old man fights the sharks but they rapidly reduce the marlin to a white skeleton. The old man, as he nears the shore, says to himself, "What beat you? Nothing, I just went out too far." If there is any flaw in the picture the film makers can say with the old man that their only fault is that they went out too far; they tried something just a little too difficult.

The Inn of the Sixth Happiness tells the true story of Gladys Aylward, a young Englishwoman who went to China as a missionary about thirty years ago. Miss Aylward, played by Ingrid Bergman, joins an old woman in a remote part of North China to start a roadside hostel that they call the Inn of the Sixth Happiness. They cater to mule-train drivers because the drivers serve as word-of-mouth newspapers throughout the area. While Miss Aylward serves them dinner the old woman tells them stories from the Bible, hoping to win them to Christianity.

The climax of the picture comes when the Japanese overrun North China. Miss Aylward leads a hundred Chinese orphans on a dangerous journey to the safety of a mission compound in the interior. During the flight the viewer might come to care about Miss Aylward because she has a hundred orphans working on her side, emotionally. But up to that point one is not emotionally involved. The writer did not take Horace's advice, "If you want me to weep, you must first grieve."

The writer must make the audience care about a character. Not to be cared about in fiction is almost as unfortunate as not to be cared about in real life. The audience must be for or against a character and it must be interested in what will happen to him; it may want to see him knighted or it may want to see him hanged, but it must care.

In *The Old Man and the Sea* the audience does care, and for that reason it has a better chance than *The Inn of the Sixth Happiness* of being dug out of the archives a hundred years from now as a sample of superb movie-making in the middle of the twentieth century.

In both pictures the principal characters were dedicated to something—catching fish or catching souls. Let us now compare two pictures in which the principal characters are involved in a love affair.

Middle-aged men have affairs with younger women in both *Middle of the Night* and in *That Kind of Woman*. *Middle of the Night* is penetrating and rings true, but *That Kind of Woman* is all surface and gives off a hollow sound. The one casts enough light into dark places to illuminate the tides of the spirit until the audience says to itself, "That is it, that is life." But the other, dealing with a similar problem, skates around on thin ice and has nothing in it of the that's-it-ness of life.

Middle of the Night is by Paddy Chayefsky and is a further indication that no one writing films today can tell about the big problems of little people as well as does Chayefsky. As in his other films—*Marty, Bachelor Party* and *Catered Affair*—loneliness is a major ingredient. Loneliness has narrowed the lives of a fifty-six-year-old widowed manufacturer and his much younger receptionist. When an October-May romance develops, the widower, long respected as a fine sensible man, is alternately elated with a new zest for life and depressed with the frustrations of self-doubt. His sister and his daughter badger him, but their indignation seems to spring more from jealousy and selfishness than from any wish to be of real help to the man. The receptionist is a neurotic young woman made even more disturbed by her broken marriage. Her confusion is compounded by her mother, a woman who has gone through life rather confused herself.

The story, then, revolves about two people trapped between the longing for love and the pressures of prudence. Like all Chayefsky films there are moments of comedy and laughter, but the over-all feeling is one of tragedy, although never despair. Each of the principal characters has a tragic flaw that has its roots, not in evil, but in a misdirected good. With Director Delbert Mann's eye for visual authenticity and Chayefsky's ear for lower-middle-class dialogue, the result is a picture of considerable artistic merit.

That Kind of Woman is about a kept woman, played by Sophia Loren, a middle-aged millionaire who pays her bills, George Sanders, and a young paratrooper, Tab Hunter. On a train from Miami to New York in June, 1944, Sophia meets Tab, bound for combat in Europe. She half-heartedly tries to discourage his attentions as he, with a lost-puppy look, follows her around Central Park, Staten Island and Grand Central Station. He haunts her during all of his last furlough in New York and does such a good job of it that he even jolts the millionaire into proposing marriage to her.

The writer has the problem of making this story seem not

only possible but probable. Certainly it is not improbable that a young paratrooper and a fiery woman his own age should fall in love. Yet the writer has not made this seem nearly so probable as Chayefsky has made his romance between a twenty-four-year-old receptionist and a fifty-six-year-old man—a romance far less apt to happen in real life. Both writers wanted to make the audience feel the waves of guilt and the waves of need rushing together. The audience cares more about what happens to Mr. March and Miss Novak than it cares about what happens to Mr. Hunter and Miss Loren; artistic truth is what makes the difference. Mr. Chayefsky has imbued his play with a certain natural grace lacking in *That Kind of Woman*.

One might find himself approving of the last ten seconds of *That Kind of Woman* and disapproving of the last ten seconds of *Middle of the Night*. In the closing moments of the one it seems that Sophia will turn her back on her kept womanhood and marry the paratrooper. In the closing moments of the other it seems that the widower may eventually marry the divorcee.

In spite of the endings, *That Kind of Woman* is not nearly so honest as *Middle of the Night*. It seems better to have a hundred minutes of honest work with ten seconds of disapproval than a hundred minutes of tinny work with ten seconds of approval tacked on the end.

Yet people who have no concern for the art of the film tend to look at pictures in parts rather than as a whole, and when they come upon an objectionable part they are likely to dwell on it until it finally obliterates the whole. They may condemn as immoral a picture which, when seen as a whole, may be making very moving moral statements.

Thus, *Man on Fire* is a most potent argument against divorce. Anyone contemplating a divorce would think twice after seeing what it does to the people, especially to the children, involved. In the closing scenes of the film, the divorced man walks along arm in arm with his secretary, giving the impression that they will find happiness together. This "happy ending" was probably tacked on because producers know that people will allow their sensibilities to be roughed up only if the saving balm of a happy ending is allowed them. People who look at pictures as parts instead of as a whole are apt to demand happy endings.

Bachelor Party had a few sequences that might be called objectionable, but the writer's moral vision was certainly accurate. The film was about some men tom-catting around town; and everything in it added up to show how such pleasures turn to dust in the mouth. To get this truth across, the writer had to show some unsavory things; he could not make his point by having the men visiting soda fountains all evening.

Subject matter, then, often blurs the vision when it comes to seeing artistic truth. A person may be so prejudiced in favor of a subject or so prejudiced against it that his judgment is blinded. I know a nun who tries to teach her art students that a well-done apple gives more honor to God than does a shoddy madonna. She tries to make them see that a first-rate artist may choose a humble subject, three apples on a table, and the result may be a painting worth having, whereas a mediocre artist may try his hand at a noble subject, a madonna, and the result may not be worth the canvas it is painted on. For artistic truth results more from *how* a thing is done than from what the subject matter is. The nun has a difficult time making this point because her students have grown up with more respect for madonnas than for apples, and they are so focused on subject matter that it is not easy for them to see that there are instances where more artistic glory shines from apples than from madonnas.

THE CELLULOID MUSE

It is a mystery why two writers can take the same subject matter and one come up with a work of art and one come

up with a work of nothing. But a clue is provided by E.B.
White in the wonderful little book, *The Elements of Style*:
"All writing is communication; creative writing is communication through revelation—it is the Self escaping into the open.
No writer long remains incognito."

Some writers escape into the open bearing gifts endowed
with a certain natural grace, things that could be inert, except
that life has been breathed into them. And then there are
writers who escape into the open proffering things like *The
Ten Commandments*.

True, *The Ten Commandments* is nothing more than insubstantial pageantry, and I did not think a film so vast and so
expensive could be anything else. But along came a genius,
William Wyler; he faced the greatest handicap an artist can
face, the handicap of too much money, and he rose above it.
He spent fifteen million dollars on *Ben-Hur* and in spite of that
brought forth a picture of artistic worth.

Ben-Hur touches the spirit because it has in it a part of the
common experience of life. This sounds silly when you recall
that it tells of a chariot race, galley slaves and a leper colony,
experiences not common to twentieth-century life. But it is
what these incidents reveal of the inner workings of human
beings that helps the audience find identification. The characters in *Ben-Hur* are moved by ambition, pride, love, hate,
compassion and repentance—emotions common to man no
matter whether he drives a chariot or a Chevrolet, whether he
is chained to a galley ship or to a bureaucratic desk, whether he
learns that leukemia has doomed him rather than leprosy. It
is the human condition that the audience vibrates to and not
to the specific experience.

Mr. Wyler told a story about the political struggle between
Jew and Roman, but he did not forget to tell it through well-defined human beings. The historian can write of a political
conflict in terms of trends and theories and come up with something worth attending to, but it will not be a work of art.

The artist when dealing with plotted narrative is stuck with concreteness and concentration of subject matter. If he deals with remote things, like a political struggle, he must bring it to such a sharp, fierce focus that the heat of it sears the souls of a few main characters and through those characters he tells his story.

In these main characters the audience should see the lights and shadows that play across the soul and sense the rise and fall in the tides of the human spirit. It is of secondary importance that the audience learns about the patch of history that those people were entangled in. If the main effort is put on history and not on individuals, the result will not be a great work of fiction, because all great fiction is primarily about individuals.

Many of the scriptural spectaculars have failed to work powerfully upon the soul because the people who made them were so excited over that pomp and circumstance which millions of dollars will buy that they forgot to develop believable characters. We can be briefly excited by spectacle but cannot really care about it for long because we cannot find identification with it. A human being can identify only with the human condition.

PAINLESS PIETY

Nuns, for example, are often presented as cute little schemers for Christ. They are so icky.* When a non-icky picture about nuns came along, *The Nun's Story,* some people resented it. Maybe they prefer the icky. They said it was not believable because the people in it were not like the nuns they knew. Kathryn Hulme answered this criticism of her book in an

---

* Since I will use the word *icky* quite often let me define it. That is icky which causes the spirit to shudder. That is icky which makes the soul feel the way the backbone feels when a thumbnail is scraped across a rough brick. When spoken, the word *icky* is usually accompanied by a hunching of the shoulders. *Icky* is not a synonym for *corny*. Icky things are always corny, but corny things are not always icky.

article which appeared in the Jesuit weekly *America* (June 27,
1959): "These critics seem to miss two points—that I was
writing exclusively of *one nun* and *her* response to her situation, and that I was describing a European order of 25 years
ago considerably more rigorous in discipline then than now,
and certainly different from many American congregations."

Those nuns *were* of another culture; a different culture
honestly rendered often is a stumbling block to the audience. I
have tripped over enough cultures in different parts of the world
to know how incomprehensible we find a culture that differs
from ours. We think there is something peculiar about it, and
often try to act as though it isn't there.

The nuns in the film, *The Nun's Story,* came from a culture
more severe than ours. The heads of families in Europe are
more severe than the heads of families we know. Governments
of European nations were more severe, and the way of living
in general has been more difficult. We would be more severe,
too, if through the centuries our homes had been in the middle
of a battle ground.

There were things about *The Nun's Story* that made me
flinch, too, because I am a person who draws back in the
presence of great discipline. I cringed at the discipline I sensed
while visiting a Carmelite monastery in this country, and I
cringed when I observed the severity of Marine boot training;
but even while cringing I admired the Carmelites and the
Marines because I know that rarely is anything extraordinary
done except through extraordinary discipline.

Fred Zinnemann, the film director, felt this same admiration
for the sisters in *The Nun's Story.* He wrote in *America* (June
27, 1959) that before he had read the book, "The idea of
convents and nuns had been quite remote and not particularly
interesting to me. On the very rare occasions when I thought
about them they impressed me as rather a lingering vestige of
the medieval past, where women tried to escape from the
world of reality for a variety of negative reasons.

"The book opened my eyes—and the eyes of millions of people all over the world—to the enormous vitality and strength and permanence of life in a religious community. Kathryn Hulme's book wipes out, once and for all, the thousand cloying sentimental notions about nuns—particularly the notion that nuns are just like everyone else, except that they are especially jolly and 'good Joes.' The book stated clearly that nuns are *not* like other people. It showed how, step by methodical step, the personalities of young girls are refined, distilled and transfigured until they are finally able to strive for the boundless freedom of life liberated from personal emotions and concerns, not beholden to time, not encumbered by and bogged down in thoughts of self. After all, it pointed out the difficulties that arise and the heroic demands that are made of those who follow their vocations."

Fred Zinnemann was not just writing those words for publication; one could believe that he really feels that way because his conviction shows up in the picture. A director, like a writer, gives himself away in his product. He could not fake the sincere sentiment found in the film. Some of the people who criticize Zinnemann do so because they do not respect sincere sentiment; their tastes run to sentimentality.

At the end of *The Nun's Story* a woman leaves the convent. At the end of *The Miracle* a woman returns to the convent. Of the two, *The Nun's Story* is the one more apt to leave the audience with refreshment of the spirit, proving that a "happy" ending is not necessary for that phenomenon. *The Miracle* is not apt to leave anybody feeling anything except fatigue and bewilderment that people should spend so much time and money and effort to create aesthetic squalor.

The importance of having faith in the thing you are working on was discussed by A. L. Vargas in *The Penguin Film Review*. He said that *Brief Encounter* is a story that is so simple that it does not even have a sub-plot and that there is nothing really exceptional about it, but its saving grace is that Noel Coward, David Lean, Celia Johnson and Trevor Howard had faith in it.

Mr. Vargas says that this picture points out once again that what really counts in making a picture is not a script "cluttered up with incident or a film audibly creaking under its burden of stars, elaborate sets, gorgeous costumes and brilliant camera work, but a story which has something to say and whose characters are not the colorless puppets of some schoolgirls' weekly, but creatures of flesh and blood, drawn in the round with all their faults, impulses, hopes and fears, like ourselves."

Why is it that *The Nun's Story* and *The Miracle,* both about women dissatisfied with convent life, should be so far apart artistically?

In *The Nun's Story* we find human beings we can identify ourselves with. As the story unfolds it reveals layers of meaning, levels of insight. In *The Miracle* we watch costumed puppets stumbling over a clutter of incidents. As the story unfolds it never goes beneath hard veneer.

The Nun's Story is a religious film, but *The Miracle* is not, even though the newspaper ads called it, "The Greatest Story of Faith Known to Our Time!" There is not a nun in sight in the documentary film, *Nanook of the North,* and in the play, *Our Town,* but there is far more religious feeling in them than in *The Miracle. Nanook,* the story of an Eskimo's life, points with pride and dignity to man's indomitable spirit, and *Our Town* is filled with reverence and awe for the wonders of God's work.

Some people may mistake *The Miracle* for a religious film because it has in it nuns, the statue of Mary and a "miracle." It takes more than habiliments to make a religious picture; it takes a religious spirit too. If habiliments were all that were necessary then all paintings and statues in religious goods stores would be truly religious. In art, to repeat, the important point is not the subject matter, but the way in which the subject matter is handled; it is not so much the *what* of the thing as the *how* of it.

There would be more artistic religious films like *The Nun's Story, Monsieur Vincent,* and *Marcelino* if there were a more appreciative audience. And there would also be more artistic secular films if there were a more discerning audience. So many people seem to shun artistic truth because they want to be fooled.

BELIEVING ONE'S FICTION

This willingness of people to be fooled was pointed up by William H. Whyte, Jr., who wrote: "It is a churlish critic who would gainsay people the solace of fairy tales. But good fairy tales frankly tell the reader that he is about to enter the land of make-believe and to relax as we go back to once-upon-a-time. Current slick fiction stories do not do this; the tales are not presented as make-believe; by the use of detail, by the flagrant plainness of their characters, they proclaim themselves realistic slices of life. They are much like the 'situation' magazine covers and the pictures of American family life featured in ads like the 'Beer belongs—enjoy it' series. The verisimilitude is superb—from the frayed cord on the bridge lamp to the askew hair of the young mother, the detail is almost photographically faithful to middle-class reality. But it is all sheer romance nonetheless; whether the scene is taking the first picture of the baby, a neighborly contretemps over shoveling snow, or a family reunion of one kind or another, the little humorous squabbles merely serve to highlight how lovable and conflict-less is the status quo beneath."

Mr. Whyte is pained by the popular preference for the icky. He writes: "Life, as it is, is beautiful enough, and one could easily gather from current reading that God is so merged with society that the two are just about indistinguishable. In an advertisement for the movie, *A Man Called Peter,* there is a picture of a man walking up a hill through some dry-ice mist. In his white shirt and four-in-hand tie, he looks uncommonly like a thoughtful young executive, but we find that he is a minister: '*He was a first-name kind of guy. . . . He was everybody's kind of guy. . . .* Every woman secretly had her eyes on him, but he had eyes for only one—Catherine—who learned from him what a wonderful thing it was to be a woman—and wrote this story that topped the nation's best-seller list for 128 weeks . . . *He was God's kind of guy.*'

"This profanity, for that is what it is, is bold, even for the popular press, but it is characteristic. God likes regular people —people who play baseball, like movie nuns. He smiles on society and his message is a relaxing one. He does not scold; he does not demand of you. . . ."*

The ad for *A Man Called Peter* is a classic example of icky writing. I said a few pages back that Zinnemann felt honest sentiment for the nuns because it showed in his work. The ad writer lacked honest sentiment and this lack showed in his work. Both Zinnemann and the ad writer reveal their attitudes. Anyone who pursues any art, even a commercial art, gives himself away.

In trying to show the difference between the film of substance and the shoddy film, I have so far selected only serious ones for comparison. Perhaps I gave the impression that art is only possible with serious pictures and that only they can give insights into life. But man is not all searching and sorrow; he has a playful side, a laughing side that needs to be explored, also. In comedy there is as much range from quality to trash as there is in serious drama. The quality comedy springs from an imagination that has freshness and refinement and the trash comes from an imagination that is fumbling and gross.

To make a paradox of it, humor is not to be taken lightly;

* William H. Whyte, Jr., *The Organization Man* (Simon and Schuster, 1956), p. 254.

it is no laughing matter. I say that because a sense of humor is a mark of the civilized man. I do not mean by sense of humor the tendency to laugh when people trip over things or bump their heads, the kind of humor found in many animated cartoons. I am sure the aborigines would laugh at those, too, because there is something not quite civilized in that laughter— listen to it the next time you are at the movies.

The civilized sense of humor is one that is tickled when it sees a sense of values go askew. It sees avarice, pomposity and ambition for the clowns that they are. It sees how incongruous it is to mix essentials with non-essentials and how irrational to mistake means for ends.

I have found that the best way to stop students from using clichés is to get them laughing at clichés and an effective way to get them to stop writing gobbledygook is to get them laughing at gobbledygook. In class we make a collection of clichés and we "translate" perfectly good English sentences into gobbledygook just to see how silly the process is.

If a writer gets the audience to laugh at a false sense of values he may help root out a few false values. If he does that, his is a noble destiny, indeed.

2. The Art of the Writer

STRUCTURE AND HARMONY
RESTRAINT
CHARACTERIZATION
MOVIES WITH A "MESSAGE"

THROUGH his work the artist communicates emotions and attitudes to another person. To "receive," the party of the second part must be capable of vibrating on the same wave length as does the artist. The artist does not communicate merely by "keeping rules." If it were as simple as that, many of the great prose works of our time would be government reports, military records and legal documents. They keep the rules of grammar, spelling, punctuation and organization, but they are far from being artistic expressions.

Sometimes an artist breaks some rules—this would score badly on a check list—but better to break a few rules and send forth a little honest feeling than to keep all the rules and have nothing happen. Of course, there are the beginners and the pseudo-artists who break rules because they do not know them, or because they are unwilling to submit to discipline, or because they are merely exuding affectation. Theirs is a sad lot, indeed: no rules kept, no artistic truth communicated. Nothing.

Let's take a look at some of the flaws that can cause a film to blur artistically: poor structure, lack of harmony, lack of restraint, shallow characterization, self-conscious propagandization.

STRUCTURE AND HARMONY

Aristotle said that any work of art should be so structured that nothing can be rightly added or nothing rightly taken away. The Greek temples had such organic unity. Nothing could be added without spoiling them and nothing could be taken away without having something seem missing. And what is good for a Greek temple is good for a motion picture.

In a motion picture no scene should be longer than necessary and no sequence should have in it more than is needed. I have heard film editors say that a few frames too many can take the edge off a scene; a few scenes too many will cause a sequence to sag, and a few sequences too many will weaken the structure of a film. Howard Lindsay in a talk about playwriting said, "Just a couple of lines can make a scene too long. Four lines make it very much too long. Six are impossible." This economy of means is a principle in all the arts.

A screenplay should move inevitably toward a climax. Sometimes this climb up the ladder—*climax* comes from the Greek word for ladder—is a fumbling effort because the development is too loose or too complex.

The Young Philadelphians is an example of a too-complex structure. Anyone who goes to see it needs a good night's sleep beforehand so that he will be alert enough to follow it through its labyrinthine ways. In two hours and twenty minutes it offers what might have been better developed into several separate films.

It tells of a sabotaged romance, a problem of illegitimacy, a social-climbing mother, a too-ambitious young lawyer, the Korean war and a murder trial. It is a sprawling picture which leans coincidence against coincidence. I would hate to try to tell the story to someone. It makes me realize the wisdom of Abe Martin's words: "Never try to describe a pain or a play."

As I think back it seems that most of the pictures I would care to see again have a simple structure: *High Noon, The Informer, Shane, Battleground, Marty, Brief Encounter, La Strada.* So many of the great ones have story lines that can be told in a few sentences. Perhaps there is some sort of law in this matter: the more complex the structure the more likely the work is to fall on its face artistically.

The structure should not be so simple that the film is completely devoid of sub-plot, although some pictures, like *Brief Encounter,* manage without a sub-plot. The sub-plot must ring just as true as the main plot. It must not live in a little world by itself but must have some influence on the main plot.

The sub-plot in *Separate Tables,* for example, seemed to get out of hand. The picture is set in an English resort hotel which caters to the lonely, the resigned and the desperate. The main plot is about an ex-army officer and a spinster. The sub-plot is about the conflicts between a divorced couple and is developed nearly as much as the main plot.

Separate Tables is a good example of a film that has flaws but is still worth seeing. Not only does it have a sub-plot that threatens the main plot, but in being adapted from stage to screen it remained rather much of a stage play—a couple of sets and a great deal of talk. I will not quarrel with this avoidance of the motion picture medium because the picture had substance. Better to say something and play hob with the medium than to bow to the medium and have nothing to say. *Separate Tables* speaks out honestly of life and is not for anyone who takes motion pictures as tranquilizers and sedatives.

A lack of harmony of parts can also spoil a motion picture. I suppose this could also be classified as a structural problem, for anyone interested in classifications.

Jessamyn West, in *To See the Dream,* said that after her book, *The Friendly Persuasion,* was turned into a movie, there was only one part in the finished film that she could not stomach—the sequence about the three backwoods girls who are man-crazy. Miss West said, "There is no humor without humanity and these girls are inhuman. Pseudo passion in red drawers . . ." Putting this sequence into the film is not quite as bad as building a tool shed against a Greek temple, but it shows some of the same lack of sensitivity. The irony of it is that William Wyler, the same sensitive artist who created *Ben-*

Hur, was guilty of this inharmonious horror. Artists, like athletes, also have their off days.

RESTRAINT

Along with organic structure and harmony of parts, the Greeks have something else to teach a film-maker—restraint. Sometimes a production is spoiled because somebody could not rein-in. This is especially true of acts of violence. Sophocles would find his artistic soul cringing at the way violence is handled in motion pictures and teledramas. The Greeks believed that it is better art to have acts of violence occur off stage, and, for the same reasons, it seems that the best way to depict violence in a movie is through what Henry James called "strong specification."

In *Shane* there is a good example of how violence can be revealed to the audience through "strong specification." In a fight between Shane and the farmer, in the barnyard, the audience does not see much of the fight, but it knows that the fight is a honey because it sees how a horse and several steers and a couple of human onlookers react. This seems better artistically than the fight Shane had with the bully earlier in the picture, which is recorded, blow by blow, right in close.

In the film, *Oliver Twist,* there is another good example of the audience learning about violence through indirection. Bill Sikes owns what is supposed to be the meanest dog in the world. When Bill begins to beat his wife, the camera holds on the dog. The audience sees the dog trying to escape from the room and knows by this strong specification that the beating is a cruel one if the meanest dog in the world cannot stand to look.

The Informer has an excellent example of how violence can be shown by indirection. When Frankie McPhillip, the hunted man, is trapped in his second-story flat, he climbs out the window to let himself drop down to the street. The camera stays inside the room and shows Frankie's arm clinging to the window sill. A rattle of shots is heard from the street. Frankie's arm lets go. That is all the violence the audience sees, Frankie's arm letting go. It is a more artistic way of doing it than to show Frankie bouncing off the sidewalk, spurting like a fountain.

In *The Set-Up*, when gangsters practically shred a prize-fighter because he did not throw a fight, the shredding is not seen. The violence occurs in an alley on to which opens the window of a jazz-joint. While the violence takes place the audience sees the silhouette of a drummer's wild actions and hears the fury of his efforts.

The violence of passion is shown by indirection in *Brief Encounter*. When the couple embraces the camera cuts away to a fast express filling the night with screeches and steam. When the camera comes back to the couple the kiss is ending, but the audience has "seen" passion and understands its violence better than if the camera had held on the embrace for thirty seconds.

Note that in all of these examples the audience knows about violence through what it *sees*, not from what somebody tells it. The main information comes through the eyes, which is good film technique, and not through the ears, which is stage technique.

I never realized how right the Greeks were about having violence take place off stage until I saw the stage play, *Time Limit*. It was marred by a glaring weakness—one soldier strangles another on stage, right down front and center, and it just does not come off.

Violence has its rightful place in drama. The objections to it are not so much objections to violence but to the lack of restraint in the telling, that is, more of an artistic objection than a moral one. If a scriptwriter took a tip from Sophocles he might improve artistically and be less apt to hear censors clamoring in the wings.

After saying that violence ought to be told by indirection, it may sound contradictory for me to say that inner conflicts should be made *visual* in motion pictures. A novel may spend pages searching a man's thoughts and walking around inside his soul, but if the novel is made into a movie, the movie ought to show by outward signs what is going on inside a man. In a play, characters may talk about inner feelings, but if the play is turned into a film, the adaptation should show those inner feelings without depending too much on talk.

Inner feelings are often described through visual symbols. In *Brief Encounter,* for example, a woman does not want to listen to a gossip and the audience is helped to share in her feelings through the use of a symbol. The gossip's mouth is shown in extreme close-up; it fills the screen until the woman is "all mouth," as the saying goes.

In *Conspiracy of Hearts* a priest tells a nun that she must stop smuggling children out of a German concentration camp. She does not want to stop, yet she is not sure that she ought to go on. The director photographed her through an iron grille and the effect is that she is caged with a dilemma.

In the same picture the nuns are praying in the chapel when suddenly the camera cuts to the bottom of the chapel door just as it is kicked open by two German officers. The explosive bursting open of the door and the sudden close-up of two pairs of boots depicts in a most effective way the Nazis' mad power and brutality. The shock of this sudden close-up causes the audience to draw back not just emotionally but physically. The recoiling is so forceful that the theater seats creak.

An exceedingly tall stool is used as a symbol of supercilious and over-powering bureaucracy in *The Cabinet of Dr. Caligari.* When Dr. Caligari goes to the city hall to get a permit he is confronted by a clerk who peers down on him from a too-tall stool. From that visual image the audience knows how the clerk makes Dr. Caligari feel.

Not long ago I saw a rerun of John Ford's classic, *The Informer.* The sound was so garbled, because of a defective sound track, that the characters seemed to speak a foreign language. Yet everyone in the audience followed the story because the picture is so filmic. Even such deep emotions as the temptation to betray, the revulsion of scorn and the nag of conscience are made visual.

In the opening of the picture Gyppo Nolan sees a poster offering a reward for his friend, Frankie McPhillip. The very way that Gyppo rips the poster from the wall reveals that temptation is whispering and that he is appalled by its voice. As Gyppo lurches away down a street as dark and foggy as his mind, a gust of wind blows the poster after him. When he stops, it leaps against the back of his legs and clings there until he fights it off. There is no need for a narrator to say that the reward for Frankie McPhillip is haunting Gyppo Nolan. The camera is saying it more effectively.

After Gyppo has told the British where Frankie is hiding, the officer who gives him the reward does not say how he feels about an informer. He *shows* it. He puts the packet of bills on a table and shoves it with his swagger stick toward Gyppo.

Some years ago there was a picture in which a middle-aged man and his wife get on an elevator and the man keeps his hat on. A few floors down a young woman gets on and the man removes his hat. Without a word, a great deal has been said about the relationship between husband and wife.

CHARACTERIZATION

With so much stress on action and on outward signs, it might be feared that character development would suffer. But if the picture is a good one, the action will reveal the characters. In the film version of *Moby Dick* the audience learns that Ahab is a tortured man seething with resentments; it learns this not so much from what he says or from what is said about him, but from what is shown on the screen. His actions give him away.

So often Hollywood stresses action for the sake of action and a great deal of surface dust is stirred up with scarcely any penetration of character. The British lean in the opposite direction, and tend to stress character development through conversation, with little revealing action, and a dull film is born.

Conflict and action in a film ought to be believable. They ought to grow out of the characters and out of the characters' environment. If the conflict and the action are not believable it is useless to argue that they should have been because the incidents were taken from real life.

A college student wrote a short story about two men who were known to everyone in a small town as deadly enemies. The men made up, unknown to anyone in the town, and decided to mark the occasion by going hunting together. In the woods one of the men was carrying his shotgun cradled in his arm when a walnut fell from a tree and hit the trigger causing a blast that killed the hunter's newly reconciled friend. Circumstantial evidence made it seem an out-and-out case of murder. In discussing this short story, a college professor told the student it was too far-fetched. He could not rightly ask the reader to believe in this freak accident. The student defended his story by saying that it had actually happened. The professor said that this only proves that life sometimes writes stories that fiction cannot dare attempt.

Coincidence is another crutch a writer should not lean upon. If a man is fleeing a lynch mob and seems hopelessly trapped the writer ought not help him escape by distracting the mob's attention with a convenient landslide or earthquake. He must somehow let the man free himself through his own devices.

In letting a character reveal himself through his actions, the danger is that the writer will draw him too simply. The writer is apt to make him all black or all white, when human beings really are varying shades of gray. A character lacking in subtlety is uninteresting, excepting to minds that lack subtlety.

The best example of screen characters who lacked subtlety can be found in the old westerns. The hero was always a clean-cut young man dressed in a light sombrero. He rode a white horse, or a palomino, or a chestnut leaning toward the light-complexioned. The heroine was usually blonde, starry-eyed and dressed in light colors. The villain, on the verge of middle-age with its accompanying puffiness, was sallow, mustached, heavy-browed and scarred. He wore a dark hat, dressed in black and rode a black or a dark bay horse.

Here were ready-made characters all decked out in symbols. The writer did not have to worry his head about revealing depths of character. The characters were as set by tradition as those in a Punch and Judy show. All the writer had to do was to figure out a knotty situation and then unravel it in favor of the white sombrero.

A character without some subtlety is almost sure to act without sufficient motivation. The audience must believe that there is a good reason for characters to do what they do. A bad character ought not to turn good too fast and a good character ought not to descend into the depth of evil too hurriedly. The classic example of insufficient motivation is the film in which the husband and wife fight like cats and dogs until they visit a little basement restaurant that they frequented in more amicable days, and a gyspy violinist plays "our song" and the audience is expected to believe that everything is going to be all right from that minute on. The writer let himself off too easily.

Minor character should be just as believable and real as the main characters. In *On the Waterfront*, the secondary characters such as the priest, the dockworkers and even the bit-part thugs, are painfully real. But the usual tendency is to give the minor characters a lick and a promise and to make them walking clichés. In *Screen Playwriting*, Lewis Herman lists the kind of clichés film writers fall into. There is a tendency to call a skinflint banker Jason, and the friend of a Brooklyn girl, Mamie. Such characters even tend to speak in clichés: "Why, you look as if you had seen a ghost. . . . I'm comin' out and I'm comin' out shootin' . . . No, don't look back, I want to re-

member you like this . . .We're through, washed up, finished,
do you hear me."

Characters that are fashioned from clichés also tend to use
props that are clichés: the steaming pan of hot water when
the doctor comes rushing into the house, the bubbling chemi-
cals in a lab scene, the horn-rimmed glasses of the secretary
which the boss removes and says, "There, you look better this
way."

MOVIES WITH A "MESSAGE"

Propaganda is something else that can spoil a film; it has
spoiled many stage plays. I do not mean that a novel, or a
play, or a movie, ought never to leave you pondering something of social significance, or some theological truth, or a
political principle. Such pondering should be the by-product;
the writer ought not aim to bring it about. As Walter Kerr
observes in *How Not to Write a Play*, "What is intrinsically
wrong with the thesis play is that it puts the drawing board
before the drama. It begins at the wrong end of the creative
scale. It begins with a firm, fast premise, achieved in the intellectual solitude of the study, and thereafter proceeds to make
all life dance to a quite debatable tune."

George Gershwin, Lorraine Hansberry and Marc Connelly
did not set out to write pro-Negro propaganda in dramatic
form when they wrote *Porgy and Bess, Raisin in the Sun*, and
Green Pastures. If they had, their work would have been icky,
and for a perceptive audience it would have scored more
against Negroes than for them. What happened was that each
writer felt the push of a story to tell or the urgency of characters clamoring to be born, and because each writer had pro-
Negro attitudes those feelings came vibrating through in the
finished work.

All this is true for religious writing too. It is apt to be less
than art if one takes an abstract dogma and tries to fashion a

story and characters to help him sell his idea. I make this point because I believe that anyone who sets out to write about religion has a special responsibility to do a good job. A poorly done religious work does more harm than good—it turns away those who have a real need and causes a general loss of respect for the subject matter. There has been enough icky stuff written to encourage this attitude. Religion deserves Grade A handling; it seems wrong to communicate it in a slipshod, tasteless way, whether it be in a sermon from the pulpit, an article in a magazine or a film on the screen. Good intentions are not enough. Pious subject matter is not enough. As Jacques Maritain has observed, piety is no substitute for technique.

I have been using the word *film* in connection with the word *art*, knowing that there may be some who object to these words sharing the same street, much less the same sentence. It used to be said that films cannot be art because they are merely photographic reproductions of the visible world. I have not come across that statement for some time; most people who think about the matter at all now agree that a film need not be a photographic reproduction of the visible world. The artist, in this case the writer, the director and the actor, can be selective; he can show some things and omit others and exaggerate and repress, all for artistic effect.

To make clear what I mean by selectivity and exaggeration, let us create a short, experimental film. We will photograph three people—an old woman, a middle-aged man and a young girl—walking down the same street. They go down the street one at a time and the camera follows each to show the street as that person sees it.

The old woman is revealed as avaricious because the bargain signs loom at her larger than life-size, and we are shown the very tension of her hands as she picks over fruit at a stand. The middle-aged man is revealed as a roué; he is over-aware of the ladies and too much taken with the wines in a liquor store window. The young girl has her mind on love; she is curious about the rings in the jeweler's shop and the furniture in the department store window.

The color of each sequence tells us something about the people. The old woman sees all in muted grays. To the roué the world is mainly gray until he looks at the sparkling wine or turns to eye a girl and at that instant the screen flares with color. The young girl with thoughts on love sees everything in vivid splashes.

The sound track helps, too. For each trip down the street it carries the same sounds, but varies the exaggeration of the sounds. The old woman hears the traffic noises with frightening exaggeration. The roué hears the click-click of high heels louder than they really are. The young girl hears the love song on a radio louder than anything else.

At the end of the block each person descends into a subway entrance. Without a word of narration the film-maker has made clear that he feels that every man walking through the same world sees it differently because each brings to it a different orientation.

If this little script sounds corny it is because I have failed in my art. But I hope I have not failed to communicate what I mean about an artist tampering with the visible world to get the effect he needs. Had the director set up his camera at the end of the street and filmed the three people walking along he would have had a visual record, but he would not have been making an attempt to establish a bond between himself and the audience, a bond of information and emotion that might bring about an aesthetic experience.

3. The Art of the Director

MOVIES THAT MOVE
COMPOSITION
THE MECHANICAL EYE
EDITING
LIGHT AND COLOR
THE SOUND TRACK

ANYONE who follows motion picture criticism finds frequent references to *the medium*—references to directors who are faithful to the medium and to films that have failed to make full use of the medium. But seldom do those who write such things bother to explain what the medium is. Books about the cinema that are written in a rarefied atmosphere do bother to explain, but they explain in a language for the initiated only, and the uninitiated put the books aside more confused than enlightened.

If I had to explain the medium in a sentence I would say: a motion picture must get up and move and not be sedentary; it must say visually what can be said visually and not depend too much on the sound track. That is not an enlightening sentence, but with a few dozen pages I hope to make it so.

Let me say first that it is possible to see many movies and still not understand this business about the medium. People who see many films prove this is possible when they come away from a picture complaining, "It wasn't like the book," or "It wasn't like the play." That might be the most favorable thing they could say about the picture. They do not seem aware that a movie has its own way of doing things, a way that is "right" for it. That is not the same way that is right for the novel, the stage play, or the live teledrama.

Jessamyn West was very aware of this difference while turning her collection of short stories, *The Friendly Persuasion,* into a movie. She tells about the process in her book, *To See the Dream.* Although she had never written a screen play, she was artist enough to see from the start that a movie ought not try to be a mirror-reflection of the novel. She felt it would be better to have a good film not faithful to the book than an inferior film faithful to the book. So she willingly made what changes were needed to make the story filmic. She felt no pangs of regret in doing it, because she believes that a book should merely serve as the idea, the stimulus, the inspiration for the film script.

MOVIES THAT MOVE

Film patrons who say, "It wasn't like the book," by way of adverse criticism, do have a feeling for the medium, but they are unaware of it. To use a wild example, if one of them went to the theater expecting to see a motion picture, but saw instead on the screen a man sitting in a chair telling a fascinating story for ninety minutes, the movie patron would feel let down "because it wasn't a movie." That ninety minutes of film may still be running a hundred years from now as an example of how a masterful raconteur tells a story, but it will not be running because it is an excellent motion picture.

To give a less far-fetched example, imagine that a movie camera is set up in row E, Center, to film a stage performance of *Porgy and Bess*. When this film is flashed onto the screen it, too, will cause the movie patron annoyance; he will sense that there is something wrong with it as a film. Were he to occupy the same seat that the camera had occupied in Row E, Center, he might come away feeling he had witnessed one of the great evenings in the history of the theater. What disappointed him as a movie patron sent him into ecstasy as a play patron because in the one instance he saw a medium misused and in the other instance a medium well used. So that is why when *Porgy and Bess* made the move from stage to screen it had to be reconceived to make it more filmic.

This matter of the motion picture medium came up in a

review written by Philip Scharper for *The Critic*. In discussing
The Bridge on the River Kwai, he said that it is a film that
may come to be regarded by another generation as a classic,
because, like every other screen classic, it exploits to the full
every advantage of the movies as a story-telling medium. It
had an excellent director, David Lean, *and "a movie camera
that moves."* "That last statement may seem redundant," he
said, "but, unfortunately, it is not. Movie makers have been
seeing too many plays and teledramas lately and have forgotten that their own medium is by far the most flexible of the
three.

"As a consequence, we have been seeing a lot of movies in
which the camera never leaves a room from start of film to
finish. This 'unity of place' is fine for a play or live teledrama,
neither of which can skip too nimbly from place to place. But
such unity in a movie represents a failure of sorts, since it
forces the camera into relative immobility. Even a good movie
like *Twelve Angry Men* (in which the camera seldom leaves
the jury room) is like having a symphony orchestra play a
composition which leaves half the instruments with nothing
to do. The symphony can play such a piece and play it well,
but it is capable of doing far more. David Lean kept the
camera busy in filming *The Bridge on the River Kwai*; as a
result, the film makes the viewer aware all over again how remarkable a medium the movies can be."

So understanding movement is one key to understanding the
medium. This movement shows up on the screen in several
ways.

For one thing, the camera moves around from location to
location: one minute it can be riding the high seas and the
next trekking across a parched desert. And once it gets to a
location it does not settle down as though it were a member of
the audience at a play. No, it keeps poking around; it is far
back, it is in close, it is up, it is down. When *Porgy and Bess*
was reconceived for the screen the camera roamed the street

of Catfish Row. It visited inside the houses. It slipped down
to the wharf and went by boat to a picnic off on an island.
And on the island it roamed around, too. But it was restrained
in its getting around; it never seemed to move just for the sake
of moving.

Another way in which movement shows up on the screen
is through the movement of the actors, They move on the
stage, too, and in the television studio, but there they are
limited in their possibilities. The stage and live TV cannot
have the flight across the rooftops, the pursuit of careening
cars down a steep mountain road and the manhunt through
the swamps. The films offer so many opportunities for actor
movement that it seems a shame not to use them; that is why
two people holding a long conversation over teacups makes
for an annoying sequence on the screen, but that same thing
happening on the stage may not be annoying.

COMPOSITION

A third kind of movement comes from the composition of
the picture on the screen. The word is used in this same sense
when someone speaks of a painting as having movement. If the
design of the picture is such that it causes the eye to move,
the movement of the eye will cause the sensation of movement
inside the viewer. Again, the stage director and the director
of live teledramas have the problem of framing compositions,
but the movie director must do so much more of it; he does
so much cutting from one thing to another, seeing things from
various distances and various angles, that his compositions
change every few seconds.

A director needs a strong feeling for design. He needs it
because the abstract form of the picture on the screen says a
good deal to the audience. The abstract form should get across
the ideas the writer had in mind.

Take the matter of lines: straight lines are masculine;

curved lines, feminine; straight lines cut by curved lines, vivacious. If the father is a man who believes in Prussian discipline his office should be designed in straight lines. If the mother is overly feminine her living room should have a curved motif —curved back chairs, round tables, oval rugs, circular bowls. If the daughter is vivacious, the lines of her room should be curved broken with straight; this gives an explosive effect. In each instance the very lines on the screen help the writer to convey something about his characters.

If the director wants a calm, quiet sequence he will compose it in long horizontals; the horizontal line is restful because the mind couples the horizontal line with the idea of repose. If the director has composed in horizontals, the editing of the sequence will have to be in harmony with the picture composition; the sequence should be edited into long, slow, easygoing scenes, no fast tempo here.

When the director wants to make an actor inspire awe he will use the vertical line to help him, the same composition that makes the Gothic cathedrals awe-inspiring. If the gang chief comes to talk terms with his victim a hoodlum stands directly behind the chief and the reinforced vertical makes the chief seem more awe-inspiring, or awful, than if he stood alone. A Grecian woman weeps and moans on the steps of the temple and when she reaches a high pitch she throws herself against a pillar and the tall vertical strengthens the scene. The matriarch is telling her relatives that she is cutting them out of her will; when she reaches the dramatic climax she goes and stands by a high back chair and the instant the strong vertical is formed even the most doltish member of the audience knows the old girl is really cracking the whip.

Diagonal lines suggest drama and force; the director uses them when he wants the screen popping with action. If the script calls for a long shot of a stagecoach being pursued by Indians, chances are the director will frame the shot so that the route of the pursuit cuts diagonally across the screen. When the town bully threatens someone, a medium shot of the bully looming diagonally across the screen is appropriate. When the camera looks at the world through the eyes of a scared, lost boy, skyscrapers, lampposts and people lean at threatening diagonals.

The way the director groups the actors on the screen also says something to the audience. If actors are grouped in a triangle or a circle they show unity of effort and agreement. If something happens to cause them to disagree, the director has them break the triangle or the circle to show in the abstract design that things are no longer going well.

The director works for a balanced screen the way a painter works for a balanced canvas and both use the same principles, the main one of which is to put a heavy object near the center of the screen and to balance it with a lighter object out near the edge. The painter has an advantage over the director, nothing in his composition gets up and moves around; a director must forever re-establish balance after movement takes place.

The new wide screens give the director headaches in composition, especially in this matter of balance. The old screens came closer to what the Greeks called the golden oblong, a proportion of approximately two to three. The new screens have proportions similar to those established by the Postal Department for slits in the mailbox: The new screens are wonderful for the panoramic, but cause real problems in intimate sequences. If in a close-up the director puts an actor's head on one side of the screen the problem arises as to what to do with all that acreage on the other side. He can fill it with stuff, but will the stuff be distracting? In *Porgy and Bess,* shot in Todd-AO, the director handled the close-up effectively, but he did not try to handle it too often. He kept the camera back a little more than usual and kept it more fluid than usual. With a fluid camera poking its nose around inside a scene he did not need as many straight cuts as usual. Maybe that is the way the large screen must be handled; too many cuts might make the audience nervous, might make the audience feel someone is blinking the lights of the universe.

When the director divides the screen into parts he must be careful that the divisions are harmonious. He avoids dividing it into two equal parts and often depends on the Greek theory of the Golden Mean. The area of the Golden Mean lies between the one-third and the one-half division marks and between the one-half and the two-thirds division marks. To give a horizontal example, if a skyline runs across the screen, the director will probably set the top of it above the halfway point but not as high as the two-thirds point. As a vertical example, if the corner of a house cuts down the screen, the director will probably have the corner cut the screen beyond the one-third point but not in as far as the halfway point; the rest of the screen will be filled with the scenery of the yard.

Anything that moves on the screen must be considered a part of the design and a force in itself. It is something else a director cannot be haphazard about because movement influences the emotions of the audience.

Suppose that a director doing a documentary film about Mexican migrant workers wants to make the point that they have a nobility as human beings and so deserve better treatment. To do this he might use two principles of movement: a movement toward the camera is stronger than one away from it; an upward movement is stronger than a downward movement. He would do well to add to this the principle that a low angle shot (the camera is down looking up) tends to exalt the subject.

He puts the camera in the center of a sugar beet row. He has a worker bend over and move toward the camera. At the right moment while still moving toward the camera, the worker straightens up. The movement forward and the straightening up, and the low angle of the camera that throws the worker up against the sky will all combine to make the audience see the field worker as noble, indeed. If combined with this are surging music and dramatic lighting, the audience will be of a mood to rush from the theater to foment a revolution among the migrant workers.

A movement across the screen from right to left is stronger than from left to right. The natural movement of the eye is from left to right, the movement of reading; if something goes contrary to this it adds a touch of drama. If a director has Caspar Milquetoast as one of his characters he will sneak him onto the screen from the left. If in the course of the movie, Caspar turns and begins to growl back at the world, the director will bring him on from the right, an entrance with a blare of trumpets behind it.

A director with a feel for movement can even use it to help balance a composition: a large quiet area on one side of the screen can balance a smaller active area on the other: twelve stolid jurors on the right might balance an active prosecuting attorney on the left.

Movement also helps the director to focus the audience's attention wherever he wants it. If he wants to call attention to one actor in a group he can have everyone stand still while that one actor makes a motion, ever so slight, and all eyes will be on him. This is a scene stealing device that actors have used against each other probably since the days of Thespis in the sixth century B.C.

Through opposition of movement the director also gets attention. If a crowd is flowing one way across the screen, a lone actor moving in the opposite direction is the one the audience will follow. Or if a crowd is flowing along and one person in it stops, the audience will immediately focus attention on the laggard. If everyone is sitting and one person stands up, he will call attention to himself.

By use of other such contrasts the director focuses attention. If one person wears a hat in a scene in which everyone else is bareheaded, the hat will focus attention. If in a scene full of dark clothes, a person appears wearing a light suit, the eyes of the audience will be on him. Directors of musicals used that trick for years; if the chorus is dressed in black, the star dancer will be in white. If a woman in a black gown is making a speech, the director may have her in front of a neutral background through most of it, but as she reaches the climax he will have her move to an area with a light background; her dark dress contrasted against the light background will make the speech seem even more dramatic.

THE MECHANICAL EYE

While talking about the motion picture medium, the camera point-of-view is something else that ought to be mentioned. In *Yellow Sky* a man on horseback is talking with a girl on foot; when the man is seen on screen the camera is down low looking up at him, a girl's eye view; when the girl is seen on the screen the camera is up high looking down at her from the man's eye view. A good example of subjective camera comes in *Bell, Book and Candle*; when the screen turns bluish and goes slightly out of focus, the audience knows the camera is giving it the cat's point of view.

In his review praising *The Bridge on the River Kwai* for its excellent use of the medium, Philip Scharper also talks about this matter of the camera taking a point of view: "The next shot is taken from the floor of the Japanese commandant's house. In the foreground the camera takes in only the commandant's legs, placed far apart, which serve as a triangular frame for the picture in the background of the British prisoners awaiting him. Previous close-ups showed the tired but strong faces of the British, above all, that of their colonel. We view them now from so far away that faces cannot be seen but only a group of dirty, ragged men in ranks. We are seeing them as the Japanese commandant saw them; nameless, faceless. The fact that he does not see them as human beings is further accented by the fact that we see only the stocky legs of the Japanese, suggesting the brute physical power he wields over his prisoners."

Closely akin to this subjective camera is the use of the camera to editorialize. The camera can do more than record facts; it can write an editorial without a word coming from the sound system. It is possible that the director will give away his feelings about such things as bureaucracy, war, wealth, poverty and divorce by the way he points his camera.

In *Ikiru*, the director shows how he feels about bureaucracy by the way he frames his picture with mountains of paper. The workers in the office seem to huddle in a prison of reports, bales and bales of them forming walls so thick that no fresh air or sunlight can come through. One office worker decides to revolt against such a stifling system. In a closing sequence he is seen standing in an ocean of paper work. Slowly he sits down and seems to disappear beneath a wave. No word need be spoken to make the audience feel the tragedy of his drowning. No editorial written against bureaucracy could carry such an emotional impact. A written editorial could quote facts and statistics and appeal to the head but it could not appeal to the heart the way Kurosawa did with his camera.

Lubitsch told something about war in the way he framed a shot. He showed a wild Armistice celebration but the gaiety of it was marred as far as the audience was concerned because the camera peered at it through the crutch of a one-legged soldier.

Eisenstein in *The General Line* tells how he feels about the rich and the poor in the way he composes a picture. A poor woman visits a rich man to borrow a horse. Eisenstein put the camera behind the rich man so that his broad, meaty back nearly fills the screen. The poor woman seen across the room is made to look exceedingly helpless by the smallness of her image on the screen. Toward the end of the sequence the rich man moves and blocks out the frame. In so doing he blots out the poor woman. The audience gets the feeling of having seen a tragic thing just as when Kurosawa's ocean of paper blotted out a government clerk.

This artistic device of giving the feeling of power and weakness by having one figure loom large out of all proportion to other figures is something that the film director has taken from the artist. Egyptian artists 4,000 years ago painted kings large and their subjects tiny. Children, before they are spoiled into thinking that art aims at exact reproduction, will draw a looming teacher and pupils that cringe before her.

I said that a director can show how he feels about divorce by the way he points his camera. This happens in a film about an American GI who brought an Italian war bride home with him. He is very much of a rat. The young woman does everything in the world to get along with him, but finally she can stand it no longer and she leaves him. As she walks from the front door and down the steps the camera is up high looking down on her, seeming to push her down into the pavement, and the street is dimly lighted and the whole scene gives off a feeling of deep sadness. The camera is saying, this is too bad, this is a tragedy, if only this could have been avoided. Now, had the director put his camera at the foot of the steps so that when the girl walked through the door it would have looked up at her, it would have exalted her, and had he lighted her so that a halo of light played about her, she would have seemed to be making an exalted resurrection from the tomb. And the audience would have felt like shouting, hurrah!

Here is a case of where the art of the scene and the morality of it got entwined. Perhaps it indicates that a moral judgment cannot be made on a film in every instance without some awareness of the art of the medium.

This matter of how a camera writes editorials also came up in Mr. Scharper's review of *The Bridge on the River Kwai*. "For example, when Alec Guinness, a captured British colonel, leads his weak and weary battalion into a Japanese prison camp, he is determined they shall be 'proper British soldiers.' They march into the sandy compound in perfect ranks, whistling a marching song, and mark time awaiting the arrival of the Japanese commandant. The effect is that of British troops from the Kipling era smartly stepping across an Indian parade ground before the eyes of visiting dignitaries. Then the camera quickly cuts to the feet of the men: dirty, bruised, bleeding, moving up and down in the coarse, hot sand—in perfect step. No need for a bystander to mutter, 'Gad, what spirit!'—the camera has already made the comment."

In general, it is good film technique to let the camera say what it can say visually. When something needs be told that cannot be told visually then it is all right for the actor to go ahead and speak. Here is a major difference between the screen and the stage. A stage play does not have the possibilities of a movie of saying things visually and so it is necessarily more talky.

EDITING

Editing is another major factor in the motion picture medium. It brings another kind of movement to the screen. The editing can be quick, staccato, lilting or lazy—any tempo the director feels best for the telling of his story. A fight sequence will be edited to run in a quick, slam-bang way; it would be wrong to have it lilting and easy going as a pastoral sequence might be with longish scenes and predictable tempo.

Editing allows a film director to work his magic in a way a stage director can barely do and a teledrama director can do only with limitations. He can take strips of seemingly unrelated film and splice them together to get a creation that is not the sum of the parts, but one that holds something greater than the sum of the parts.

Early Russian directors did a great deal of experimenting with putting different strips in juxtaposition with each other to learn what emotions they would evoke. One experiment went something like this; a director took three strips of film, a man looking with horror, a close-up of a bowl of soup, and a close-up of a woman in her coffin. When he spliced the look of horror to the bowl of soup the audience laughed. When he spliced the same look of horror to the dead woman, the audience felt a chill. In both instances the look of horror was the same, but different things in juxtaposition with it caused the audience to move from one side of the emotional spectrum to the other.

This brings to mind the story of the actor who during the filming of a Biblical picture was told to look off right and register horror. He did just that, but did not have the slightest idea of what the horrible sight might be. He went to the theater a year later to see the finished picture; he saw his look of horror and then onto the screen popped Salome holding a tray with the head of John the Baptist on it.

A director can take bits of unrelated reality and through editing create a new reality all his own, a film reality. He is something of a builder and his art is not unrelated to that of architecture. When a builder takes stone, brick, wood and steel and assembles them according to a plan, the result is more than the sum of the parts; it is a creation with an emotional appeal that the parts did not have when they were delivered to the building site.

A few more examples of how a director creates an illusion through editing might help to give additional insight into the medium. In the film, *Some Came Running*, a young man walks to the window of his hotel room and looks out. At that instant the facade of a jewelry store pops onto the screen. The audience says to itself that the jewelry store is right across the street from the hotel. That is the film reality, but the true reality is that in Madison, Indiana, where the picture was filmed, the jewelry store is several blocks from the hotel. Through the juxtaposition of two pieces of film the director makes the audience believe what he wants it to believe.

In the same picture, two actors are riding along the street in a car. They look off to the left and a sign telling of a centennial celebration pops onto the screen. The actors in the car never really saw the sign, it was painted after they had left Madison.

Another good example of creating a film reality comes from the same picture: a young man walks across the porch of a mansion and steps through the front door. The instant he steps through the door the camera cuts to the inside of a lovely room. The audience believes that this lovely room is inside the mansion. What really happened was that the exterior of the mansion was filmed in Madison, Indiana, and the young man entering the room was filmed on a sound stage in Hollywood, two thousand miles away, and a month later.

The chariot race in *Ben-Hur* runs nine minutes on the screen. The filming of it took three months. So it is really more of a film editor's victory than a victory of the white horses over the black horses.

The bullfight sequence in *The Brave One* proclaims the art of the film editor and proves that a director can "make" an actor. It also indicates that there are stories the motion picture medium can tell far better than the stage or the live teledrama.

In the film a Mexican boy raises a fighting bull that turns out to be very brave. He is heralded as the greatest fighting bull in the country and he is sent to Mexico City to face the moment of truth with the greatest matador. There is a production problem if there ever was one—the greatest bull meets the greatest matador and they put on the greatest fight of all time. This is something that cannot be rehearsed, especially since the matador is not a matador at all but an actor with a good profile. So thousands of feet of film were exposed at bullfights and then the director and the film editor sat down together to create the doggonedest bullfight in the history of man.

With a snipping here and a snipping there they built the

sequence. A muleta flicks, a bull's head blurs, a matador postures. A hoof paws the earth, a cape twirls, a crowd cries, "Ole"—many bulls, many matadors, many crowds brought together there on the editing table and made to seem as one.

The bull, created from many bulls, gave a performance that might have won him an academy award as the best male performer of the year, had he been eligible. Through the art of directing and editing it is possible to take a performer not much more talented than a fighting bull and have him give a superb screen performance. This miracle is not possible on the stage or in the live teledrama because there actors are required to give a sustained performance.

An Italian bricklayer's face happened to catch the fancy of Vittorio De Sica; the director took the man who had never had a bit of acting experience and made him the star of *Bicycle Thief*. Right after World War II, Italian directors were filling their films with non-professionals and their product then was far better than it is now.

If an actor can do for only ten or fifteen seconds at a time what the director tells him he may end up on the screen giving a superb performance. And he gets several tries to get it right, for it is not unusual to retake a scene a half dozen or a dozen times. The scene in *Teahouse of the August Moon*, wherein the Army Colonel says to the natives, "Let me tell you about democracy," had more than fifty takes. With many takes to choose from the director and the film editor pull out the best and edit them to the proper tempo and so build a performance.

Even if an actor, through years of experience on the legitimate stage, is capable of giving a sustained performance he finds this skill unneeded while making a motion picture, because pictures are filmed all out of sequence for the sake of convenience and economy. Suppose that a picture opens in a railroad station. A wife is seeing her husband off to war. It ends in the same railroad station when she greets him on his return. Rather than shoot the beginning and go away to come back three months later to shoot the ending, the director will shoot beginning and ending while his unit is set up in the railroad station.

I hope I have made clear why a director more than anyone else connected with motion pictures puts his stamp so completely on a film. He is not depending on the actors to give him a sustained performance; rather they are depending on him to take the many bits of effort that they have given him over a period of months and use these snippings to build a creditable performance. That is why people who know something about motion pictures are more apt to ask of a film "Who directed it?" rather than "Who's in it?"

LIGHT AND COLOR

Up until now we have been looking at the director's use of camera and have said nothing about that important person, the cameraman. A director who has a good director of photography is wise if he gives him a fairly free hand. Such excellent directors of photography as James Wong Howe, Robert Surtees, William Daniels, Gregg Tolland, Arthur Miller, Jack Cardiff and Lee Garmes have given invaluable help to directors in picture composition, movement and lighting.

Lighting is an art, and more than anything else separates the first-rate from the second-rate cameraman. A good script, good direction and a fine performance can be spoiled by insensitive lighting. There are cameramen who develop feeling for movement and composition but who never seem to master the lighting. Incidentally, this ability to describe the subject in terms of highlights and shadows is also the hardest to come by as far as the portrait painter is concerned. The cameraman, like the portraitist, paints with highlights and shadows.

Lighting can make irregular features pleasing and harmonious features homely. It can make a face full or lean, old or young, haggard or radiant. Each year when my students go to a television studio for a demonstration I am impressed anew with the possibilities of lighting. The director takes a student about twenty years old and has him sit on a high stool in the center of the studio. The director lights the student until he looks much younger than he really is; he shines with an angelic naïvete and you can practically see the fuzz of adolescence softening the line of his chin. As the class watches on the monitor, the director changes the lighting and gradually the student grows older and older, innocence deserts him and before long he is a hardened criminal.

Lighting can also change the personality of interiors and landscapes. It can make them happy or sad, cool or warm, inviting or unattractive.

To observe the effect of lighting, notice how that part of the path covered with the lacy pattern of leaf shadow is more charming than the part of the path in the full glare of the sun. White houses that may lack personality in the cold, gray light of winter often take on distinction when their façades are covered with the leafy shadows of summer. Light and shadow speak a visual language.

Color is another language the director needs to understand. It says things so strongly that we use colors in figures of speech: "I get the blues when it rains . . . She was green with envy . . . He saw red."

Some writers who dwell on the aesthetics of the cinema have said that they wish color film had never been invented. They feel it has hurt the art of the film. I feel that color hurts the art of the film only when it is misused. Color in itself is good, and anything that helps the artist communicate is worth having around.

Some pictures are best in black and white—*High Noon, Third Man, On the Waterfront.* But some pictures, *Lili, Gigi,* and *An American in Paris,* would be impoverished without color. Perhaps we can make a rule of thumb out of this: screenplays that deal with dire things are best shot in black and white; those that speak of bright things are best shot in color.

Exceptions immediately leap to mind. *The Nun's Story*

dealt with solemn matters and yet was effective in color because Fred Zinnemann used color creatively. He used it to make visual the feelings of his main character. While Sister Mary Luke is in the cloister all the colors are muted grays, but when she reaches the Congo colors burn with such intensity that they almost sear the retina. When the nun returns to the cloister the colors are muted again, but the audience knows she still has fierce color burning inside her.

Vincente Minnelli used color creatively in *Lust for Life*. He used the colors and the compositions of Van Gogh, and what could be more appropriate in telling the story of the artist's life.

In the *Wizard of Oz*, Victor Fleming used color with imagination. The scenes of the real world of the Kansas prairies are in black and white, and those of the make-believe world of Oz are in color.

Just as the director can heighten the effect by following a quiet sequence with a lively one, he can also create an emotional response by using colors in juxtaposition. If he wants to slam the audience with a red sequence he can increase the jolt by putting in front of it a green sequence. The complementary green will cause the red to seem even redder than it is. This is using color to create a certain impression or to give vent to an expression. It is certainly not using it for the sake of realism.

The writers who fear color fear it because they think it will try to push the cinema too close to realism. But it need not. A full palette need not force an artist into realism. Painting would be narrowed indeed if an artist were limited to black, white and gray.

THE SOUND TRACK

Sound is another thing that some writers who philosophize about the cinema wish had never been invented. Much of this annoyance with sound goes back to the early talkies. The very word *talkies,* never heard any more, indicates that producers in the early thirties were enamored with the new possibility and often used sound for the sake of sound. Several things happened right after *The Jazz Singer* was released in October, 1927. For one thing the whirr of the camera motor was being picked up by microphones and so the camera was immobilized inside a soundproof booth; it could no longer get up and get around with much ease. Insensitive mikes helped immobilize actors, too. Then there was the rush from Broadway to Hollywood of writers, directors and actors, all stage oriented, who tried to turn motion pictures into stage plays on film. The dialogue ran in a constant stream and the close-up, one of the most effective devices of film, was used less and less.

In the thirty intervening years, directors have learned to use sound rather than abuse it. The camera is now soundproofed, so that it need no longer be confined in a booth. Mikes are more sensitive and the technique for their use has been developed so that actors are no longer such slaves to them. Most important, writers, directors and actors have learned that even with the addition of sound the motion picture medium is still different from the medium of the stage.

It is paradoxical that although the stage depends on sound more than does the motion picture, it is the motion picture that offers the more possibilities for its use. This is indicated by looking at a few titles in a studio's sound library—horse running on dirt, horse running on cobblestones, cow mooing, engine starting, roar of a waterfall, gurgling brook, and on ad infinitum.

Sound can make an artistic contribution. The creaking of the giant tree in the cemetery sequence in *Great Expectations* adds greatly to the mood and sets up the audience for a jolt a few seconds later when the gigantic man grabs the little boy.

A film called, *Have I Told You Lately That I Love You?* has a sound track that is a little work of art. The picture, a satire on our push-button age, was done by a student at the University of Southern California as his thesis in cinema. A father, mother, and a little boy move through a day bombarded by communication. The first things to communicate with them in the morning are the alarm clock and the radio. The day is filled with recordings, telephones, auto horns, intercom systems, sirens, public address systems, dictaphones, television, and a dozen other things that assail the eardrums. Commercial communication so crowds the lives of this family that they lose the ability to communicate with each other. The sound track is the master stroke: it is filled with clichés from many fields—newscasts, business letter dictation, soap operas —all run together so that you keep thinking you are about to make sense of what is being said, but you never do. Although this is a story about sound it is a proper use of the motion picture medium because no other medium could tell this particular story so well.

Those two delightful short French films, *The Red Balloon* and *The Golden Fish,* were shot silent and music was added later. They tell their stories so visually that peoples of every tongue can easily follow the story. Yet the added music is helpful; it heightens the charm. It was not selected just to fill the sound track; it is functional because it contributes to the emotional effect.

Those who yearn for a silent screen argue that sound leads to realism and to a corresponding lack of artistry. Adding possibilities for realism is not bad in itself, just so the artist accepts the responsibility of selecting the aspects of realism he will use. Anyone completely anti-realistic would have to be against the silent films, too, for a bunch of Keystone cops running down a street is not without touches of realism. Anyone completely anti-realistic would have to settle for those abstract films that pop non-representational forms on and off the screen, and that send squiggles and lines and blobs running and scooting and bouncing all over the place. Some of those films are enjoyable and bring a real emotional experience, but to settle for them alone would limit the medium unfairly.

Sound is often abused. Because sound is possible the writer sometimes forgets the visual possibilities of the picture in motion and turns his thoughts to talk. Sometimes the characters are so busy talking about things that happened that the audience does not have a chance to share in their happening.

Many sins have been committed in the name of background music. Some directors seem to fear a little honest silence; their phobia is akin to that of the advertising man who fears a little white space. A director who loves a loaded sound track does not have enough artistic sensibility to deal with the job before him. When someone is faced with an artistic task too much for him, he will usually try to make quantity take the place of quality. To know when to stop, to know when to rein in, to have a sense of restraint—those are the marks of the master.

It is easy to recall films in which sound was happily used: The zither theme in *The Third Man;* the haunting trumpet in *La Strada;* the violent percussion in the opening of *On the Waterfront* foretelling terrible things; the exaggerated ringing footsteps of the police in *The Third Man* telling of the trapped feeling that clutches at the villain.

Each year the music on the sound track is being better integrated with the sequence on the screen because more and more music is being written especially for films. Even when an old song is used—such as *Waltzing Matilda* in the picture *On the Beach*—the arrangements are handled to integrate perfectly with the film.

This better integration is also taking place in musicals. It used to be that the songs and the story line rarely "met." But in such latter-day musicals as *My Fair Lady, Gigi* and *Guys and Dolls* the story line dovetails with the songs like cogs in a piece of machinery.

Porgy and Bess did not reach the screen until twenty-five

years after it was written, yet it held up because George Gershwin was a pioneer in the movement to coordinate music with story. When he went to South Carolina to listen to Negro jazz, spirituals and folk songs he did not take anything intact. He feared he might end up with songs pasted onto a story line. So he wrote his own spirituals and folk songs and his strong sense of unity made the music and the story line all of a piece.

Film directors with a strong sense of unity are always concerned with making the story and the music work together. At last they are listening to the Greeks: everything should be so constructed that nothing can be rightly added and nothing rightly taken away.

4. The Art of the Actor

ACTING: TRAUMA OR TECHNIQUE?
THE REAL AND THE ROMANTIC

THE most valuable asset of a motion picture actor is an unusual ability to project something toward, even into, an audience. What is projected is a certain quality—Spencer Tracy exudes the smell of masculinity; Sophia Loren, the scent of the tigress and Jessica Tandy, the lavender of good breeding.

John Crosby, the TV critic, wrote of Lilli Palmer; "Hers is an exquisitely modeled face abounding in sharp corners at the tip of the nose, the edge of the lips, the edge of the eyes; a cat-like, alert, vixenish face which instantly commands attention. In fact, everything Miss Palmer does commands attention. She endows with great, though mystifying importance, her walk, her movements, her gestures."

This magnetism that lifts what is done and said above the dull, is not a gift limited to one walk of life or to any level of education. I have found it most often among Negro laborers and least often among the well-educated of every race. There is a touch of earthiness about it that is educated out of some people. I do not pretend to understand this mysterious alchemy, this form of creative chemistry. It is a blending of body and soul—too much body, and the quality is smothered by animality; too much soul, and it goes off into the fine mists of the ethereal.

What I am trying to say is that the important thing in a screen actor is what he exudes as a person; his skill as a performer is secondary, for the very way in which movies are put together does not allow him to display a great skill. On the stage the exuding of a certain quality of personality is not nearly so important as the ability to create a performance. Helen Hayes exudes no special quality as a person, but she can create through her skill as a performer any impression she sets out to create. Perhaps this is why she has been far more successful on the stage than in the films.

ACTING: TRAUMA OR TECHNIQUE?

By now it should be evident that the film lends itself to a different kind of acting than does the stage. It is more reined-in. The subtle expressions of Alec Guinness on the screen would be lost on a stage audience. If some of the exaggerated expressions on the stage were filmed in close-up, they would cause the audience amusement; witness some of the old silent films in which stage technique was used in front of the camera.

The stage developed two principal styles of acting and both have been carried over with adaptations to the films. The styles, neither well-named, are the *Method* and the *technical*. The Method is recent, and reached our stage indirectly from Stanislavski; the technical is probably as old as the art of acting.

To understand the Method we have to turn back more than eighty years to Ibsen's revolt against the romantic drama of his day. Plays of the Romantic Period were flamboyant and stylized; they were usually concerned with people in high places, and if not in high places, at least in high spirits. A good example of Romantic drama, although it was written nearly a generation after Ibsen's revolt, is *Cyrano*. With his *Pillars of Society* in 1877, Ibsen started a new trend in playwriting. He is the father of what is popularly called "realistic drama"— the play that deals with the little problems of the common man and domestic life. It seems to rip one wall from the side of a house, usually the most decrepit house in the neighborhood, and lets you peek at what goes on inside. A few years later Chekhov took up realistic drama and the trend was in full swing.

As this new drama became dominant, Stanislavski, the director of the Moscow Art Theatre, sensed a need to develop a new style of acting which would be in harmony with the spirit of the play. He developed a style that is popularly called realistic. His system became so widespread that at one time it looked as though the slouch might replace the stride, the grunt the soaring speech and the torn T-shirt the flowing cape.

Stanislavski started his system toward the end of the last century, but it was not really adopted in this country until the 1930's. During the Depression, when nearly everyone in the theater was out of work and not inclined to be in a mood sympathetic with the Romantic Period, Elia Kazan, Clifford Odets, Stella and Luther Adler and others formed The Group Theatre. They sat around and talked Stanislavski's ideas, and from those talks evolved a system which they called, the Method. To this day professionals still say, "Do you use the Method?" or "Is he a Method actor?"

A Method actor psychoanalyzes the character he plays. He does not want to act the part, he wants to *be* the part. He is interested in improvisation and the inspiration of the moment. With a stage full of Method actors, improvisation frequently flits about like a bat in a ballroom. A technical actor, on the other hand, will go on night after night giving the same part the same interpretation. He is not so concerned with self-expression as with giving the audience the presentation of a character as the writer wants it given.

The difference between the Method and the technical might be made clear by naming a few proponents of each school. The Method was popularized by Marlon Brando, Julie Harris, James Dean, Shelley Winters, Kim Hunter and other members of the younger set. The technicians are Alfred Lunt and Lynn Fontanne, Cyril Ritchard, Helen Hayes, Maurice Evans, Laurence Olivier and John Gielgud. Some of the Method actors, like Julie Harris, have leaned toward the technical side and some of the technical actors have picked up a few shoulder shrugs from the Method, so that the no man's land that once separated the two schools is now rather crowded.

If one wants to study the two styles of drama that bring out two styles of acting—one "realistic," the other "romantic"—two good films to see are *On the Waterfront* and *Red Badge of Courage.* These pictures are similar in that both deal with violence and the problems of courage and fear in the face of violence, but there the similarity ends. *Waterfront* is realistic in handling and *Red Badge* is poetic in handling. Each bears the stamp of an excellent director—Elia Kazan directed *Waterfront* and John Huston directed *Red Badge.* The story behind these two pictures casts some light on why they are different and why they had to be different.

Budd Schulberg got the idea for *Waterfront* from a series of newspaper articles describing working conditions in the New York harbor. He was so shocked and stimulated by the series that he decided to do a film on the subject. This journalistic inspiration is evident throughout the film and fits well with realistic handling. Even in getting his material, Schulberg worked like a journalist. He spent six years in researching the subject and in writing the script. At one time he spent every day for five months sitting through long, and often dull, hearings conducted by the Crime Commission. Sometimes he dressed like a dockworker and hung around harbor bars getting inside the problem.

This could scarcely lead to anything but a realistic script. When time came to shoot it, Schulberg and Kazan decided that since it was so realistic in feeling it ought to be made visually as realistic as possible. They decided to shoot every inch of film on location: for home scenes they rented a flat, for church scenes they went to a church, and for bar scenes they took the camera inside a bar. They won the Academy Award for the best sets without even building a set.

They also made it a point to get along with as few professional actors as possible. For dockworkers they used real dockworkers, and for strong-arm men they used ex-prizefighters Tony Galento, Abe Simon and Tammy Mauriello. The professional talent was so well cast that practically every professional in *Waterfront* was nominated for an award. It ended with Marlon Brando being named best actor of the year and Eva Marie Saint best supporting actress. Lee J. Cobb, Karl Malden and Rod Steiger, Method actors all, were in the running for supporting excellence. The picture won eight Academy Awards, tying the record set by *Gone With the Wind,* a picture that required a non-Method way of doing things.

The story behind *Red Badge* is different. The inspiration for the script was Stephen Crane's Civil War novel, *The Red Badge of Courage.* As you watch the picture you are aware that you are enjoying fiction; there is no trace of journalistic realism.

Huston did his best to bring out the poetic mood in the novel. He even tried to get the soft focus and diffuse lighting found in Brady's Civil War photos. He framed each scene with as much care as an artist puts into the composition of a painting. He rehearsed and rehearsed and shot and reshot. He shot a ratio of forty to one; in other words, for every forty feet of film shot only one reached the screen.

This contrasts with Kazan's system; who shot far less film and often avoided too much rehearsal hoping for spontaneity and the actor's inspiration of the moment, a tenet of the Method system. In the scene where Brando and Steiger are riding along in a car saying bitter things to each other, Kazan did not have them memorize the lines. He told them the ideas he wanted expressed and let them do it their own way. As you watch the scene you sense they are working it out right then and there and are not speaking from memory.

Waterfront and *Red Badge* represent two schools of motion picture making that are far apart. I doubt that Huston would be attracted to the *Waterfront* script or that Kazan would consider directing *Red Badge*. The followers of Kazan, the Method group, consider Huston's way of doing things old-hat, and there are those on Huston's side, the technical group, who look down their lenses at Kazan and his colleagues.

Waterfront and *Red Badge* both deserve to exist, and they prove that good work can be done on each side of the fence. Of course, horrors have been turned out by each side, indicating that you cannot judge a picture by the school it came from; you can only judge it by how it stands or falls of itself. Just as in painting, the important thing is not whether a picture is Renaissance, Baroque, Impressionist, Expressionist or Cubist, but how it stands or falls of itself as a work of art.

Two of my four favorite directors, John Huston and John Ford, are of the old school, and two, Elia Kazan and Delbert Mann, are of the new. I cherish each because each contributes to a need I feel inside myself.

I have need for Huston and Ford because I am struck with the plaintiveness of the line in T. S. Eliot's poem, *The Love Song of J. Alfred Prufrock*: "I have measured out my life with coffee spoons." So much of life is measured out with coffee spoons that it is good to have film directors who measure out life with heaping liberality. Huston and Ford are men born outside their time; they have an Elizabethan bigness, a romantic swoop and flair which we should all come in contact with sometimes; it is needed for a balanced diet of the spirit.

I have need of Kazan and Mann because I am impressed with the truth of another Eliot line: "This is the way the world ends / Not with a bang but a whimper." The whimpering side of life is what Kazan and Mann are interested in interpreting. They are not at home with drama larger than life. They like to examine the small side of life and realize it so thoroughly that the audience smells sweat and tastes grit. This is also something we need to face up to for the sake of a balanced diet.

THE REAL AND THE ROMANTIC

We need two ways of directing and of acting to keep in harmony with two kinds of writers—those who lean toward romanticism and those who lean toward realism. No writer, and no human being for that matter, can long balance on the sharp edge of reality. To put it cruelly, each must live to some extent by illusion or by disillusion. The problem is not to go whooping off too far in one direction, as some romantics do, and not to go snarling off too far in the other direction, as some realists do. A writer ought to hover near reality so that he will show humanity as frail but not irredeemable, and life as difficult but not futile.

Those who dislike the Method style of acting are annoyed with the kind of play that brought the style into being. The Method fits the trend in drama that speaks of the problems of "the little man." When plays were about kings and queens and the beautiful and the articulate, the grand style of performing was appropriate, but now that plays are about ugly butchers and unloved dockworkers and others who limp along humble paths and are not too articulate, the Method seems necessary. Homely actors are finding their place in the sun; the beautiful used to be the only ones who had a chance to star. (Even animated cartoons are getting around to the homely theme; I saw one about two outcast skunks who found each other and were lonely no more.)

A book about playwriting says, "The more tremendous the obstacle the more dignified the play. If a new suit of clothes is all that prevents a man from winning a woman, the matter is not of great moment—but if he has to overthrow an empire to get her, the play is apt to be important." Those words were written in 1927 when more writers felt that way than do today. Writers now realize there is as much potential drama in the story of a man breaking his heart to win a freckle-faced girl as there is in a man breaking his heart to win a kingdom. In both cases he breaks the only heart he will ever own. The story of the freckled-faced girl really tells the audience more about life because it happens more often and is within the audience's realm of recognition. *Bicycle Thief* showed the audience that the loss of a bicycle can cause as much suffering as the loss of an empire. A bricklayer and an emperor can suffer only so much, and when their capacity for suffering is brimming, each is deserving of compassion.

I am all for the Method and all for the plays that glorify "the little guy." But I also see the dangers; I see that writers can get the idea that people in high places, once honored in fiction, ought only be presented as vile creatures. *Executive Suite* makes men at the top of a corporation very unsavory. *Patterns* gives the impression that in the business world one mounts by walking roughshod across the souls of underlings, by stomping them so hard that hope will never grow again. A *Leaf out of the Book* asks you to believe that a cutie is on her way to becoming vice-president in charge of promotion because she is ornamental. *A Woman's World* gives the impression that top-echelon promotions come through wifely connivance instead of through aptitude and experience. If business executives were really such buffoons as they are made in *The Solid Gold Cadillac,* the country would have been bankrupt long ago. Military fiction has its inadequate Captain Queegs and detective fiction its immoral Mike Hammers, and a staple ingredient of situation comedies is the head of the family who is soft-brained and bumbling.

I am not arguing against any one of the particular dramas mentioned above. What concerns me is the pattern, the attitudes, the atmosphere. There are weaknesses in high places, but too much harping on them begins to resemble an adolescent revolt against authority more than it does art.

Men should not be condemned who have a little more intelligence, imagination and articulateness. And a man with a couple of extra dollars in his pocket is not necessarily a dishonest heel.

I hope I have made it clear that I am all for both the Method system of acting and for the technical. I am in favor of glorifying both the little man and Mr. Big, and when necessary, of pointing a finger of shame at both. The final test of a film is not its style of acting or its subject matter, but what it does to the audience. Did the audience, at least the alive members, find some illumination? Did anyone leave the theater feeling a heightening of the senses that comes with an artistic experience? Did some members of the audience find something haunting their spirits long after the final fade-out? Or did the film bring the depression that comes with pseudo-insights, or, just as bad, the shallow cheer one finds in advertisements? Or perhaps nobody felt anything, except a cold draft across the spirit.

It is dangerous business for a critic—or the viewer—to align himself too completely with one artistic style; it blinds him to the virtues in others. He might prefer one style, but he must never forget that art wears many faces. In the plastic arts we have seen Impressionism, Expressionism, Cubism and other "isms" come and go and each has left behind some wonderful things. And some junk. The drama is no exception to this inexorable rule of change. Every style runs its course. The Greek theater wore out in less than three generations. The Elizabethans and the best-known period of the French drama lasted less than two. All of which leads us to realize that art is not only long; it is also wide.

5. The Grammar of Film

THE CRAFT OF THE CAMERA
THE STRUCTURE OF A SEQUENCE
THE ELECTRONIC EYE

WE CAN attack from another direction this problem of what is "right" for the motion picture medium if we approach it through motion picture terminology. Even the study of definitions can give insight into how a motion picture gets its effects, especially how the camera, the very heart of the medium, goes about doing what it has to do.

The words *scene* and *sequence* have been used many times in these pages, and now we are in a better position to define them. The word *scene* in motion picture production does not have the same meaning as it does in play production. In a play, "Act I, Scene Two," might refer to a block of material that runs for twenty minutes on the stage. In a movie a scene runs only a matter of seconds. Sometimes it is just a flash on the screen of a second or two and rarely does it run more than twenty or thirty seconds. My guess is that the average movie scene is about ten or twelve seconds long.

The best definition of the word *scene* that I have come across is, "That which takes place in front of the camera from the time the camera starts until it stops." This is clumsy-sounding, but about as close as anyone has come to an adequate definition.

In a shooting script each scene is numbered:

> 57. LONG SHOT—CAMPSITE—NIGHT
> A campfire is burning in a canyon. Three men sit close to it.

58. MEDIUM SHOT—PARKER, WOOD, OWENS
They huddle as close to the fire as they dare. All seem dejected.

59. CLOSE-UP—PARKER
His head is lowered but he takes a quick furtive glance at his companions.

The director would shoot the first of these three scenes by having the camera set up perhaps fifty feet from the campfire. An assistant would hold a slate in front of the camera with Scene 57, Take 1, printed on it. The camera would run a few seconds and then stop. The director might shoot this scene from several different angles and later decide which is most effective. The camera will move in closer for scene 58 and again this will be slated. For scene 59 the camera moves close up to Parker. The scene number on the slate will remain 59, but the take number will change as the director shoots Parker's furtive glance in several different ways.

All of these scenes are part of a sequence, referred to as the campsite sequence, which runs for, say, seventeen scenes. This is followed by the bank robbery sequence of thirty-seven scenes.

By now it might be unnecessary to give the definition of *sequence*: "A group of related scenes that develop the story in a given location."

If a sequence runs for quite a number of scenes, chances are it will have within it *cut-ins* and *cut-aways*. A cut-in is some detail of the main action inserted in the sequence and a cut-away is a shift of attention from the main action to a related action.

These definitions can be made more clear by looking at the way films handle a football sequence. The game is the main action. A cut-in would be a close-up of a foot meeting the ball. A cut-away would be a scene of the crowd cheering. The cut-away might be to a related action outside the stadium; the star player fights his way through traffic having escaped from the gamblers who had kidnapped him.

The cut-in and cut-away are sensible devices because that is the way you see things in life. If you attend a talk you do not just see the speaker, who is the focus of attention; you also watch him pour a glass of water, that is a cut-in, and you look about at the audience, that is a cut-away.

The cut-away is useful to the director in helping him give the impression of a lapse of time. If a steamboat is churning down the river heading for a landing, it will probably use up three minutes of screen time if the camera holds on the boat from the time it turns from midstream until it reaches the landing. The director knows it is not worth that much time, so he cuts away from the boat to a bunch of loafers lolling on the levee. A few seconds later he cuts back to the boat which is just about ready to throw out its first rope. The director has saved almost three minutes and has helped create a mood and a setting for the landing.

The cut-away, on rare occasions, is used to prolong time, especially when it is combined with a certain overlapping of scenes in editing. I recall how this is done in a fact-film about the treatment given to a crippled boy. In the climactic sequence the boy puts his crutches aside and walks across the living room into the encouraging arms of his parents. To help the audience feel the way the boy feels—that the living room is very long and that the time it takes to cross it seems an eternity—the director stretched time. By cutting away from the boy to the parents and by cutting back to him at different angles and by having the action in each scene slightly overlapping the director makes more screen time elapse than was actually needed for the boy to make his painful walk across the room.

With the words *scene* and *sequence* explained, we can move on to the key to all motion picture camera work, the basic shot sequence. The basic shot sequence is long shot, medium shot, close-up, and re-establishing shot.

The *long shot,* also known as an *establishing shot,* shows the main object in relation to its general surroundings. The *medium shot* shows the main object in relation to its immediate surroundings. A *close-up* includes only the main object and usually only the important part of it. The *re-establishing shot* reorients the audience as to what surrounds the main object. All of this might best be understood by looking at a simple sequence:

Long shot—The main street of a western town. At the far end of the street a man is riding in on horseback. He is leading a pack horse.

Medium shot—Man on horseback and pack horse continue along main street.

Close-up—Pack horse. A man is strapped across the saddle.

Re-establishing shot—The horseman continues along street and dismounts at sheriff's office.

If ten excellent cameramen were given this script each would shoot the scenes a little differently. Some of the long shots would be longer than others and some of the close-ups would be closer than others. The choice of high and low angles would vary. Each cameraman would put his stamp on his way of telling the story as Rouault and Cezanne put their stamps on their paintings.

The basic shot sequence is not something cameramen agreed on behind closed doors and decided to foist onto the public. It is a sensible, inevitable way of developing a story visually because this, too, is the way you see things in life. If you enter a room full of people and are looking for one person, you first get a long shot of the room, an establishing shot. You see what kind of room it is and what kind of people are in it. You narrow your search to small groups, medium shots. When you see the person you are looking for you go up to him, a close-up. If you are with him for a time, you do not continue the close-up, but eventually look around the room, a re-establishing shot.

Sometimes, for a good reason, the camera starts with a close-up, moves back to a medium shot and then moves back to a long shot. This is especially useful for shock effect. A close-up of a limp hand with a revolver beside it; a medium shot of a man sprawled on a shabby sofa; a long shot of the sofa in a gritty room. The reaction to this close-up is different from what it would have been had the camera started with a long shot and worked in to the limp hand with the revolver. The audience would have been more prepared for it this way.

Sometimes a sequence will open with a close-up if the director wants to make a special point of something by placing it in juxtaposition with the final close-up of the preceding sequence: A sequence ends with a drooping flower in a pot. We know from what has gone before that the flower is on a fire escape in a slum. The next sequence opens with a close-up of a lush flowerbed, and when the camera pulls back the bed is found to be in a pretentious garden. The director might be making a social comment; he might be saying that some have to be content with this, while others have this.

It is in the close-up that film technique departs most from that of the stage. In the opening sequence of *The Bridge on the River Kwai* the quick cut to the close-up of the bruised feet has an impact the stage cannot get, at least not in that way. So a writer and a director who are conscious of the motion picture medium make good use of such devices peculiar to the medium.

THE CRAFT OF THE CAMERA

The usual way to move a camera so that the image on the screen changes is to stop it and pick it up and carry it to the next set-up and start it again. But there are some movements that will change the image on the screen while the camera is still running.

The *pan* is one such movement. In the pan the tripod remains in place, but the camera pivots from right to left or from left to right. The camera should not pan without reason, and the most usual reason is to follow movement. Amateur photographers are often pan-happy; they use a camera to spray a scene the way they use a hose to spray a lawn. This technique abounds in home movies.

In the *tilt shot,* the tripod remains in place but the camera pivots up or down. A tilt also should not be used without good reason.

A *dolly* means that a camera rolls on its tripod toward the subject or away from it—a dolly in and a dolly out.

In a *travel shot,* sometimes called a *follow shot,* a camera moves parallel to the subject—when, for example, the camera follows along beside a runner or keeps up with a speeding train or a runaway stagecoach.

In a *zoom shot,* the camera remains stationary, but seems to move toward or away from the subject because of the action of a zoomar lens. This shot is often seen in a televised baseball game; the camera holds the batter in a medium shot until he gets a hit and then the audience feels it is zooming to the outfield, riding the wings of a jet in pursuit of the ball.

A *boom shot* is the most fluid of all camera movements. For it the camera is mounted on the end of an hydraulic arm so that it can dip toward the subject and pull back and pan and tilt and dolly and travel from all angles.

The camera *angle* speaks to the audience. In a high angle shot the camera is looking down on the subject which usually has the effect of making the audience feel superior. In the low angle shot the camera is down, looking up at the subject and the audience tends to feel inferior. In a flat angle the camera is about on the same plane as the subject.

To understand how the camera angle helps the screenplay

writer to tell his story, imagine an argument between two men. When the camera is shooting the winner it should be down low looking up at him, throwing him up against the sky. When shooting the loser it ought to be up shooting down, pressing him into the earth. So as the film cuts back and forth between the two men one is up and one is down, visually.

A good motion picture should tell its story so visually that the audience will have an idea of what is going on even though the sound system fails.

Optical effects—dissolve, fade, wipe—also say things to the audience. They are transitional devices used to move from one sequence to another.

In the *dissolve* the last scene of one sequence melts into the first scene of the next. In the case of the wilted flower in the pot and the flowerbed, the wilted flower and the flowerbed would share the screen in a brief blur, and then the wilted flower would disappear to allow the flowerbed to come into full focus. One knows that there has been a change of time or place or both; it is like coming upon a new chapter in a book.

In a *fade* the screen darkens until it reaches black and then grows lighter until a new scene is visible. The audience accepts this as a way of saying there has been a great change of time or place or both. If a sequence in India is followed by a sequence in the United States a fade comes between the two. If an old man is talking about times past and there is a flash back to the days of his youth a fade properly separates the present from the past.

A *wipe* is another transitional device that helps lead the audience from one sequence to another. With it one scene is rubbed off simultaneously with the appearance of another. Sometimes it looks as though a windshield wiper is moving across the screen; sometimes an iris forms in the center of the screen and seems to explode into a new scene. Wipes are not often used now because they are too artificial; they tend to call attention to themselves, and technique which points to itself is a serious flaw. A work of art does not exist to show off technique.

A *straight cut* is used to get from one scene to another within a sequence. This is made merely by splicing two strips of film together. Sometimes there is a dissolve from one scene to another within a sequence to give the feel of time passing. In *Ben-Hur,* two men float on a piece of wreckage after the sea battle. They sight a ship at a distance that would take at least half an hour to cross, but a dissolve brings the ship to the piece of wreckage in a second.

THE STRUCTURE OF A SEQUENCE

All of this brings us to the important matter of the build-up of a sequence. It is build-up that puts a director to the test. How does he use his long shots, medium shots, close-ups, high and low angles, cut-ins and cut-aways to give variety, interest and dramatic effect to a sequence? If he uses too much build-up the sequence drags; if he uses too little the sequence is never realized and falls limp.

The best way to study build-up is to watch for it in films that are simple and severe in structure. Here the build-up must be just right or the whole story goes off into a fine mist. Notice how interesting things can be when the camera gets inside a sequence and pokes around looking at things from different distances and from various angles, calling the attention here, focusing attention there, and now back here again.

Films like *High Noon, Shane* and *Men in War* depend on build-up more than most because of their simple structure. *Men in War* follows a platoon through one day in Korea. The platoon runs into a series of incidents, most of which can be described on the screen without words, but not without build-up, lest it fall flat. In the mine field sequence there is little motion as a soldier probes for a mine with his bayonet while his companions stand around sweating it out. This lack of movement must be compensated for with dramatic build-up. If this sequence happened on a stage it would have to be accompanied by excited talk, because a soldier lying on his stomach in the middle of the stage, poking into the dirt while his companions stand in the background would not seem very dramatic. But a camera can take the audience right in on the operation. It shows a close-up of the bayonet slipping gently into the earth; a close-up of the tense face of the prober; a cut-away to the other soldiers filled with anxiety.

The better a director is at build-up the less he depends on dialogue and the more credit he gets from the critics for turning out a product that makes use of the medium. But the director cannot move his camera around inside a sequence for the sake of movement only; he works under limitations. For instance, if a camera shoots a scene from inside a room showing an old man sitting in a rocker next to a window, the next scene cannot be shot from outside the window looking in just because the director thinks the camera ought to move or because he feels the window panes will form a pleasant pattern on the screen. He can only use that shot if it is motivated. One way it can be motivated is to have someone approach the window from the outside; then the camera looking in would see the old man from the visitor's point of view. And of course that motivation is not valid unless the visitor has something to do with the development of the story. "Everything must be so constructed that nothing can be rightly added and nothing rightly taken away."

THE ELECTRONIC EYE

In trying to make clear what the motion picture medium is, I have made comparisons between it and the stage and have slighted television. When I did mention television I spoke of the live teledrama, and meant the stress to be on the word "live" because it is in live productions that television can best be spoken of as a medium. I am going to make some exceptions to that statement almost immediately, but what I am trying to emphasize is that when a television station runs a motion picture it is using television as a means of distribution and is not testing the medium for any artistic merits it might have in itself. With the increased use of film and video tape, television may eventually stop exploring the possibilities of live productions.

It would be unfortunate if live television disappeared completely. George Schaefer, one of TV's best directors, has explained why he prefers to direct a live show to one taped or filmed: "A live drama," he said, "brings to television all the excitement of a first night in the theater. The actors, director, cameramen, and all concerned with the production feel a spark and glow they cannot possibly capture in a filmed play. The players know they have to go on the air that night, and for the best part of 90 minutes really act. There is no stopping or turning back. It is the same sort of performance they would be giving on the stage. If anything, they have to be a little more alert in TV drama."

As a medium, television falls somewhere between the motion picture and the stage. In its movements and in its change of location it cannot range as widely as the film, but it can range far more widely than the stage play. Since the live teledrama is a continuous, sustained performance, like the stage play, its scenes and sequences cannot be as complex as those of a film. For example, a fight sequence in a live teledrama cannot be as slam-bang as a fight sequence on a film, although, of course, the fight sequence could be filmed or taped and inserted into the live teledrama. Perhaps it will eventually be decided that the most effective use of the television medium is live in combination with taped or filmed sequences.

Television as a medium is sometimes very like the stage and

sometimes it is more closely related to the film. Its affinities to the stage were clear during the television production of *Our Town* because it used props without sets, something the film of that play could not have done. But in the live television production of *For Whom the Bell Tolls,* because of its realism and movement, the medium seemed remarkably like that of the motion picture. Perhaps that is the glory of television—it can couple the live immediacy and excitement of the stage with some of the mobility of the film. Those two great advantages probably tell much about television as a medium.

Even a film made for a television screen should not be made quite the same as if it were being done for a theater screen. The very size of the screen tells the writer and the director to be wary of such insert devices as the letter, the newspaper headline, the telegram. The size of the TV screen also suggests that a long shot should not be as long on a TV film as one that will eventually be projected on an area the size of a Pennsylvania barn. To look at it the other way around, perhaps close-ups can come at more frequent intervals on a TV screen than screens of vast acreage.

Perhaps the small screen lends itself to one kind of story and the large screen to another kind. Paddy Chayefsky thinks television best lends itself to intimate dramas—"intimate" meaning minutely detailed studies of small moments of life. TV plays, he says, ought to dig deep below the surface to show more profound truths of human relationships. Such intimate drama on a gigantic screen runs the danger of looking silly; the big screen is the place for stories of heroic size, for the panoramic, for the tremendous crisis.

As I watched Art Carney's performance in the television play, *Call Me Back,* I wondered if it could be equally effective on the stage or on the screen. Probably not. Here is a case of what Chayefsky calls an "intimate drama." For an hour, Carney was the only person on the screen. As Tom O'Neill, an alcoholic, he suffers so from loneliness that it has become a disease. His wife has left him and has taken their daughter with her; his friends shun him, and he has drunk himself out of another job. For an hour he sits on the couch with a bottle of whiskey and a telephone. He makes call after call as the audience watches the final disintegration of a human being. No, I do not think this particular play would hold up on the stage or on the movie screen, but it is effective television.

So much for this matter of the medium. I hope I have made clear what critics mean when they say that a certain writer ignored the medium or that a director was faithful to the medium. I hope I have more than suggested that when someone walks away from a motion picture complaining that "It wasn't like the book," or that "It wasn't like the play," he does not exactly deserve a gold star in criticism.

6. The Films of the Future

THE NON-FICTION FILM
THE USES OF ADVERSITY
FACT-FILMS AND FICTION

TELEVISION was supposed to be the death of the motion picture. Some statistics make this sound true: *Newsweek* reported that the motion picture audience dwindled from sixty million a week in 1946 to forty million a week in 1958. Even without knowing that statistic you sense that something is wrong when you walk into a theater. It is so lonely inside. As an old trouper used to say in the dying days of vaudeville, "You can shoot a bull moose in the mezzanine and nobody will discover him for a week."

The decline in attendance caused a decline in the number of feature productions, from 600 in 1946 to 229 in 1959, again according to *Newsweek*. In spite of this statistic more film footage is exposed each year than ever before. Television hurt the movie houses and the Hollywood feature film, but it has been a real boon to motion pictures as a whole.

THE NON-FICTION FILM

Television did motion pictures a favor when it found a home for the non-theatrical film, sometimes called the documentary, the fact-film, the idea film, the non-fiction film. I will use these terms interchangeably, although I know the word documentary at one time had a definite meaning now blurred by such imprecise use as I am guilty of.

Before World War II only about 5,000 fact-films existed, but in 1959 alone about 7,300 of them were produced. Of course, most of these were never shown on television, but it was television—and the growth of audio-visual education, and the growth of adult education, and the rising interest of business and industry in such films that have set the cameras whirring all over the country. But television, I feel, did the most for documentaries because it helped the audience acquire a taste for them; they do seem to be among those things that need an acquired taste—like olives, and Scotch and the prose of Joseph Conrad.

Motion picture houses offered no encouragement to documentaries. Robert Flaherty, the father of the documentary, found this out to his sorrow, for there were few outlets for his pictures when, about forty years ago, he started a revolt against the Hollywood way of making movies. He felt it was wrong to coop up cameras inside studios; he believed cameras should roam the world recording true life against real backdrops. Flaherty felt that make-believe life acted out in front of painted sets was the province of the playwright, not the film-maker.

Flaherty, a burly, rough-hewn man, was one of the great free spirits of our time. He felt sorry for anyone who trod well-beaten paths and merely filled life's span; he preferred to live life as a glorious adventure. He felt, like Whistler, that most people tend to live less than life size. He believed that to live a little larger than life is poetry.

Flaherty spent a year and a half in the Arctic making *Nanook of the North.* He went to the South Seas for *Moana,* to a barren island off the coast of Ireland for *Man of Aran,* and to India for *Elephant Boy.* He roamed the southwest part of the United States for *The Land* and the Louisiana bayous for *Louisiana Story.*

Flaherty made only about a half dozen films from the time he started in 1919 until his death in 1952. He worked with maddening slowness; he would not be rushed; he had to steep himself in the locale. He felt he had to know the hearts and the minds of a people before he could get them down on film.

Hollywood, with its production-line methods, had no patience with such loving care. Some producers sensed that documentaries were worthy of attention, but they also sensed, and probably rightly, that the public had no interest in nonfiction so long as heroines slithered and heroes breathed hard and chorus girls tap-danced up and down long flights of steps.

Flaherty lacked interest in the man-made spectacle and got his effects through his deep feelings from simple things. His films have tactility; they make the audience "feel" things in the mind. When Nanook licks an icy knife blade the audience flinches, and when the gale lashes the sled dogs everybody in the audience feels the wind searching through his bodily joints right down into the crevices of the soul.

Of the medium, Flaherty said, "Motion pictures are a very simple form of communication, you cannot say with them as much as you can say with the written word. But what you can say you can say with more conviction."

When he made *Nanook,* Flaherty started something that has been a real contribution to television. It may be that TV's greatest contribution to date has been the continuing development of the documentary technique.

One of the reasons television gave the documentary such a good send-off was the excellent series called *Victory at Sea.* The series won so many awards and attracted such favorable attention that it started the television industry and the public thinking favorable thoughts about documentaries.

Victory at Sea portrays naval operations during World War II in twenty-six half-hour episodes. The film used in the series was selected from sixty million feet made available by ten governments. Much of the film was captured from the Axis powers, and so the audience gets, literally, both sides of the picture. The first of the series shows a Nazi U-boat attack on an Allied convoy, filmed through a German sub's periscope. The second episode is the attack on Pearl Harbor seen through Japanese eyes.

The late Henry Salomon, Jr., the originator, writer and producer of the series, had prepared himself by working for five years as an assistant to Rear Admiral Samuel Eliot Morison on the fourteen-volume *History of the United States Naval Operations in World War II.* Salomon also spent two years viewing and editing the film. All this care gives *Victory at Sea* an extra dimension when compared with *Crusade in Europe* and *The Big Picture,* two similar documentaries which are anything but slipshod, but which lack that touch of magic that the sea series has.

A remarkable thing about *Victory at Sea* is that when it is rerun on a television channel it usually draws twice as many viewers as it did on the first run. On the second go-round one might find the music and the narration too urgent, too voice-of-doom like, although both are impressive at first hearing. The music for the series was written by Richard Rodgers. Sound effects are made to work in harmony with the score— airplanes, for instance, always fly in F Minor.

Another series that did much to explore the possibilities of the documentary and to give it status in television was *See It Now.* The program was produced by Edward R. Murrow and Fred W. Friendly, two men who have done as much as anyone to try to give television some altitude.

Murrow expressed the ideas out of which the weekly documentary grew: "Television is not, to my way of thinking, primarily a means of communication. It is rather a means of transportation, whereby its vast audience can be instantly transported to the various world stages where history is being enacted."

In the first minute of his first show, Murrow proved that he meant what he said. He had a camera on the east coast and one on the west coast, and by using a split screen he put the breakers of the Pacific on the left side and the waves of the Atlantic on the right, and as they seemed to swish together, Murrow said, "These are strange times we live in. These are times a man can sit in his living room and see the waters of the Pacific and of the Atlantic at the same instant."

Such dramatic imagination was characteristic of the series. Each program usually had two documentary films with Ed Murrow commenting and tying things together. Fred Friendly assigned his directors and camera crews to get "the little picture" for documentaries, believing that through the little picture we come to some understanding of the big picture. On one occasion, Friendly's men captured the little picture by following a pint of blood from the donor's veins in this country until it flowed into a soldier's veins near the Korean front. Through that little picture they brought the audience more insight into the big picture of war.

After *See It Now* was dropped, Friendly began a series called *CBS Reports,* much like the old series except that it delves into subjects more deeply. *CBS Reports* is one of the most important projects ever undertaken by television because it is something of a trial run, and, if successful, may lead to more of the same thing in years to come. One important thing about it is that it is being sponsored by a new type of advertiser.

Usually documentaries are sponsored by steel companies or aluminum companies or other organizations whose products are at least one step removed from the ultimate consumer. They are bought as institutional advertising, for prestige, and not because the sponsor hopes the audience will hurry out after the program to buy the product. But the sponsors of *CBS Reports* are using a direct sell. So if the series attracts an audience and if the audience buys the products, other informational programs may move from institutional advertising to direct sale advertising and become financially more attractive for networks to produce. Another important thing about *CBS Reports* is that it is being given a chance at prime evening time. So often documentaries have been relegated to Sunday afternoon and had no chance to prove whether or not they have audience appeal.

THE USES OF ADVERSITY

While television encouraged the non-theatrical film it was, in a way, doing the theatrical film a favor. At least from an artistic point of view it was, because it was forcing Hollywood to try harder. Serious film makers knew how true were the words of David Sarnoff, who as president of NBC said: "In a competition between mediocrities, the free (meaning free of charge) must win." Serious film makers realized that to hold their own against television, the free mediocrity, they must move their product to higher ground.

Not long ago television did a one-hour film describing what its rival is doing to rise above mediocrity. Three things were pointed that might help films artistically and, it is hoped, may help them regain some of their lost stature. (1.) The rise of the hand-made film. (2.) The tendency to do more on-location shooting. (3.) The development of the long film.

During the program David Selznick said, "The future of the industry is in the hand-made film, the picture on which one man works for as long as it takes to make it good." This is a departure from the production line, a system under which there was not much chance for artistic expression on anyone's part. Many of the best films are now made by independents. Independent producers might rent studio facilities and use the distributing system set up by the studios to get their films around to the theaters, but the important thing is that they do the picture the way they want to. It is their baby and so they are more likely to handle it with loving care. When the people doing a picture are sold on it as something worth doing they bring to it an enthusiasm and an inspiration that is lacking on a production line.

Later in the same program, Joseph Mankiewicz, who

directed *The Quiet American,* was asked if he could not have done that picture just as well if he had made it for a major studio instead of doing it independently. He said that a major studio may not have allowed him to say the things he wanted to say, because the major studio "with its need to play it safe, might not have thought it polite." He believed that television had made Hollywood realize that it is not an industry but an art form. "In the near future, pictures will continue to be made but not anywhere near the numbers of the past. Nor will they be seen by the vast audiences of before. They will be made by individuals who have something they want to say."

As for the matter of more on-location shooting, Selznick remarked, "To use an old phrase, I think the world should be the stage for motion pictures." That sounds remarkably like what Flaherty was telling producers a generation ago when they were having their own way, no TV competition, and so did not have to try to find out what is best for motion pictures. Some of the on-location shooting is encouraged by low production costs abroad and by tax structures, but even many of the films made wholly in this country are being done more and more frequently on true-life sets.

The long film is getting more serious thought in Hollywood's effort to rise above mediocrity. Length in itself is not a virtue. A long mediocre film is much worse than a short mediocre film because when you come away from a long one feeling stiff and sore, "like a horse what's been rid hard and put up wet," then all the world seems disenchanted, a feeling often brought on by witnessing an inartistic effort. But a long film often has a better chance of being substantial than a short one. If you were ever in little-theater work you know it is more difficult to find a good one-act play than a good three-act play. You may have noticed on television that the hour and the hour-and-a-half dramas tend to be better than the half-hour dramas. The playwright needs to have the audience attend to him for a sizeable length of time if he is to create a believable situation and develop it properly. If he must telescope things he may end with all surface and no depth.

Hollywood has turned out some BIG pictures with more acreage than art. It has also turned out some sizeable ones worth sitting through—*Giant, War and Peace, Moby Dick, Around the World in 80 Days, The Big Country, Porgy and Bess,* and *Ben-Hur.*

This movement toward the special film is in line with something Jesse Lasky predicted a few years ago. He said the theatrical film can stage a comeback only if it is so exceptional that it will mold new habits for movie-goers. He said Hollywood should make fewer and better pictures and show them in more glamorous theaters. He thought the public needed to be encouraged to take "an evening out" attitude toward motion pictures as it always has toward the concert hall and the stage. The only loser in the long run would be the popcorn-littered movie house where the manager refuses to help make movie-going something special.

Lasky realized that producers cannot expect people to dress-up, make arrangements for a baby-sitter, drive to town, pay a parking fee, buy tickets and drive home again unless their is something special on the screen. For all that time, money and effort they must get something considerably better than the things beating against the TV antenna. Films need not be three or three-and-a-half hours long to make an audience feel it is having an evening out. Such more usual-length pictures as *Diary of Anne Frank, The Nun's Story, The Bridge on the River Kwai* and *The Mouse That Roared* are of a quality that makes the audience feel they were worth the time, money and effort it took to attend.

Hollywood has tried to make a comeback across several routes other than quality. It has tried gimmicks, advertising that misrepresents and imitations of success. As for gimmicks, as soon as the producers felt TV's threat they began tinkering with large screens, both flat and curved, 3-D, tricky lenses, new sound systems and, latest of all, AromaRama that lets the audience smell what is shown on the screen.

Mind you, I am not against technical advancement. I am not one who writes about the cinema bemoaning the coming of sound and of color, wishing, at least so it seems, that nothing had changed since the filming of *The Great Train Robbery*. I am not against technical advancement, but I realize that in the arts it is always dangerous to assume that bigger and better equipment is the answer. Show me a photographer who is always thinking he could take better pictures if he had a better camera and I will show you a tinkerer, not an artist. If better equipment were the answer, Sunday painters would be the great artists of our generation because they usually put their hopes in fancy equipment, far fancier than a professional artist owns. A pencil and a typewriter manufacturer have run ads showing their products endorsed by successful novelists, knowing that some people believe they will be able to write enduring prose if they use approved equipment. A real artist tends to resent equipment; he wants the finished product to reflect him, not the equipment. It is the same way with money: an artist does not feel put upon with a modest budget; he may even fear a big budget, fearing the finished product might be the money talking, not himself.

Gimmicks will not save a poor idea any more than they will make an inartistic person more artistic. All they do is put a newer, or a slicker, finish on vulgarity. Junky music or inane dialogue are not lifted one degree by stereophonic sound. The 3-D pictures could not blame their ineffectiveness on 3-D; they would have been just as unfortunate in 2-D.

Advertising that misrepresents is no more helpful than gimmicks in bringing stature to theatrical films. Even pictures of the highest calibre are sometimes besmirched by the ad writer. An ad for *Lust for Life* showed Van Gogh ripping the clothes from a model, but there was no such scene in the film.

How could anyone guess from the ad that here was an educational film that teachers might encourage students to see?

I saw *Ikiru* at a press preview, and when it opened at a theater a few days later I was startled by the looming poster of an exotic dancer. Even the restrained New York *Times* ran the picture of the dancer as the only illustration in the film's ad. The dancer is on the screen about thirty seconds in a film that ran for 8,400 seconds. Her part is so minor she is not even in the credits. Yet the promotion is built around her.

The dancer is not in the film for publicity purposes but to help Kurosawa say what he wants to say: the sleazy side of life hangs heavy on the spirit. Just as the dancer in *Bachelor Party* was not there to help bring in the crowd, but to help Chayefsky, too, say that the sleazy side of life hangs heavy on the spirit. In both instances, when the dancer is removed from the context she becomes something to leer at and not something that helps an artist say what he needs to say.

Just looking at it as a money matter, ads that misrepresent must in the long run be bad for business. The ad that makes a movie seem salacious when it is not will cause some people to stay away who might otherwise have attended; so the box-office suffers. A promise of the salacious will bring some people inside, but when the film fails to produce what it promises those patrons will feel cheated, and surely dissatisfied customers do not make for good business. Like gimmicks, ads that misrepresent will attract the curious for a time and give business false courage. But the curious are not noted for loyalty; for all they care movies can go to the limbo reserved for Davey Crockett hats, hula hoops and other things that thrived briefly on fickle fancies.

The imitations of success are especially painful to those of us who see quite a few films. Let one picture make money and it will scare up a whole covey of like things. Imitation is deadly business in any art form. An artist wants to see the best that is being done. He may admire it, even envy it; such work will inspire and even influence his way of doing things and this is good, but conscious imitation is not.

After *Shane* had proven itself a money-maker, *Time* magazine reported that Hollywood was working on ten imitations. At one time there was a run on films lecturing fathers on how to get along with their sons; I recall *The Lonely Man, The Young Stranger* and *Fear Strikes Out* as harping on this. Then motion pictures and television had a cycle dedicated to the proposition that show people are not lovable; two films in this cycle were *A Face in the Crowd* and *The Great Man.* Along about that time there was a brisk marketing of underwater films. In quick succession I saw *Secrets of the Reef, Silent World* and *Secrets of Life.* This was especially painful for me because I am not much captivated with skittering schools of fish, underwater music and writhing octopuses. Another trend was in films that ought to have carried Sigmund Freud's name in the credits; pictures like *Lizzie* and *The Hanging Tree* had their roots in the clinic. After attending several of those I know how the psychiatrist felt when he wrote a letter to the New York *Times* complaining he no longer enjoys the theater; he used to go to refresh the spirit, but now he feels he is still in the office compiling a case history.

Television did the theatrical film-maker another favor by encouraging him to use documentary technique for some fictional films. This added another string to his bow. For a long time the documentary was a pure form as factual as an encyclopedia piece, but eventually it became involved with fiction and semi-fiction. TV encouraged this involvement with such programs as *Dragnet* and *Medic.* The fictional film, *On the Waterfront,* has a strong documentary flavor, a technique that seems right for that story. Had *The FBI Story* stressed documentary handling a little more, and dropped the family life of Agent Hardesty, it might have been still better—and less sticky on the edges.

FACT-FILMS AND FICTION

The documentary technique usually gets into fiction via crime stories, but it has its place in other stories, too. *Lovers and Lollipops* is a good example of its use in developing insight into an intimate aspect of human relationships. The picture was more like a well-done home movie than a highly polished theatrical film but this "home movieness" seemed the inevitable way of telling this particular story. Such feeling of inevitableness of technique, the feeling that this was the one and only way to do it, is one of the marks of art.

Lovers and Lollipops tells of an attractive but not at all glamorous young widow who starts keeping company with a man her own age, a man nice enough looking but not one who would cause anybody to look twice when he walks through a restaurant. The only hindrance in the romance is the widow's seven-year-old daughter. The problem is one of acceptance; the man must accept the child and the child must accept him. The widow finds it easy to accept them both and must suffer through some uneasy moments.

If the picture had fallen into the usual clichés, it would have made the child excessively cute or excessively brattish, but the child is believable and understandable, and anyone who knows children will respond to the honesty of the portrayal. Such sequences as when the man helps the little girl get her becalmed sailboat from a pool, and when he reads to her, and when he takes her shopping are so very real, and yet they could have been so very phony. It is realistic in the best sense of the word. So often when the word realistic is used in fiction it is a synonym for depravity. This film is realistic in that it paints a picture of an aspect of life as not all sunshine and not all thunderheads, but dark days mixed with bright days, the usual shadings of human experience.

Lovers and Lollipops was made entirely on location in New

York and is another example of the extra dimension of believability that comes when the camera goes forth to meet life instead of waiting inside a studio until life is brought to it. The picture was probably made on a shoestring; maybe a hundred-thousand-dollar shoestring, but still a shoestring as far as film-making is concerned. Morris Engel and Ruth Orkin produced, wrote, filmed and directed the picture. The tragedy in film-making is not that we have so many mediocre pictures; the tragedy is that when a fine film like *Lovers and Lollipops* comes along it finds such slight appreciation and even scorn.

While television was popularizing the documentary, audio-visual education and adult education were growing and doing their share to help develop a taste for all kinds of non-theatrical films. The universities and colleges got so interested that they began making films, a further decentralizing of film production. The University Film Producers Association was formed a dozen years ago and has since done much to improve the quality of non-theatrical films. For a week each summer, producers from fifty or sixty universities gather to show some of the films they made during the year. From eight in the morning until after midnight they grapple with the problems of film production. They sit through about forty pictures, fourteen discussion periods, two business meetings. Mealtimes are given over to committee meetings.

The titles of their pictures tell something of what they are up to: *Storytellers of the Canterbury Tales*, University of Southern California; *Cancer Quest*, University of Wisconsin; *Asexual Reproduction*, Indiana University; *Correlating Music with Social Studies*, University of Iowa; *Modern Irrigation Efficiency*, University of California.

A fifteen-minute period of criticism follows each picture. The writers, director and cameraman are asked to defend why they did what they did. Such sessions have paid dividends. In the early years the University producers were captivated with technical matters—makes of cameras, lighting equipment, film stock, lenses, filters, lab processing, sound systems—but at recent meetings the talks have centered more on the heart of the matter, the script. Most of the discussions now revolve around the question: Was the script worth it?

Some of the teaching films even have wit and charm. Yale did one showing a beginning chemistry class how to make a wash bottle, not a likely subject for wit and charm; but the music and the narration made out of what could have been a dull few minutes something that not only delighted the audience, but really taught what it set out to teach.

Another teaching film that caused excitement because of its charm and imagination was *The Seven Bridges of Koenigsberg*, a five-minute animation. This visualization of a classic problem in topology proves that a lively imagination can bring to pass wonders; it can even make the presentation and solution of a mathematical problem a thing of beauty.

The story goes that in the olden days in Koenigsberg, the townsfolk used to amuse themselves on Sunday afternoons by trying to see if they could stroll across each of the town's seven bridges without crossing the same bridge twice. Nobody had ever done it, and yet nobody had ever proved that it could not be done. A mathematician decided to use his head instead of his feet. The little animation presents his reasoning visually. Incidentally, he concluded it was impossible to cross each bridge only once; to do that the people of Koenigsberg would have to build themselves one more bridge.

In time the universities might improve non-theatrical film standards still more. They can help mainly through the students they train. If they enter the field of motion picture production with good academic backgrounds, lively imaginations and cultivated tastes, their graduates will help to raise standards. The schools must never forget that motion picture standards are not advanced by people getting into film-making just because they know how to tinker with fancy equipment.

And now that the word *standards* has come up again, let's

look at it in light of the non-theatrical film. Practically everything said so far about the fictional film can also be said about the fact-films, and nearly everything said here about the fact-films can be applied to the fictional film.

I am going to discuss the fact-film in some detail, because it is the side of motion picture making that is growing. The attention it gets is not in proportion to its growth. So much attention goes to fictional films that the public might get the impression that the non-fiction film is not worthy of attention, that it has no possibilities as art.

I suspect that I helped give that impression in the first chapter when, in speaking of the "texture of life," I used only fictional films as illustrations. Flaherty's *Nanook of the North* would have served the purpose as well. In this picture, journalism and art blend. It is journalism because it is a superb job of reporting the life of the Eskimo and it is art because it shares an aesthetic experience. The journalist and the artist are more closely related than either admits—each has the problem of communicating through selectivity and arrangement.

The fact-film is an excellent vehicle for helping us live beyond what our own living can be. Most of the time we learn about life from day-to-day living, bumping up against life, getting bruised and scarred, and, occasionally, exalting in the glory of being. But sometimes we learn of life through a shared experience. If the person who brings us the experience is an artist, he makes us suddenly realize some aspect of life with an acuteness and a clarity that does not come with day-to-day living.

Of the 7,300 fact-films made last year not many can be called works of art. But not a very high percentage of the 229 theatrical films released in 1959 were of that calibre, either. And not many of the 12,000 books published last year rate the title of "work of art." This is true of every human work. Of the millions of bowls of soup served last year how many were inspired? The bridgework of many dentists could be better. Most haircuts given last year did not rise above mediocrity. Mediocrity is a fact of life. Though it is part of man's fallen nature and will always be with us, still it is a part of every man's destiny to transcend it.

Television would do well to keep befriending non-theatrical films. It should give even more attention to them than it has in the past, and, for the most part, leave theatrical productions to the movie houses. If TV is ever going to amount to much it will have to use information and education, rather than fiction, as the basis of programing.

Having all networks dedicated to commerce and show business can only lead to trouble. Show business is interested in creating illusion, and only at its best does illusion illuminate. The medium will become a factory for fabrications, an industry for illusion, and reach the point, as was brought out in the TV quiz hearings, where it is difficult for the audience to separate fact from fancy. Too much dedication to commerce is dangerous because commerce is mainly interested in selling things and that often means attracting a crowd, no matter what. This, too, brings to mind evidence given in the TV hearings.

Having the networks oriented to show business and commerce is as frightening as having all newspapers exist mainly for ads and entertainment. It is even more frightening because there are only so many possible channels on the air, but newspaper presses can be manufactured ad infinitum. Many television writers must feel that they are just putting down words to fill the lapse of time between the beer lyrics and the headache relief cartoon. As a reporter said who worked for a paper that was too much dedicated to commerce and entertainment, "I feel like I'm just writing to fill up the white space between the ads and the comics."

I doubt that television will ever stress information and education, the area of the fact-film, but whether it does or not it will not be the death of motion pictures. Radio was supposed to kill newspapers, magazines, books and phonograph records. Television was supposed to kill radio, newspapers, magazines, books, phonograph records and motion pictures. But in the field of mass communication nothing ever kills anything. Each medium shifts to new ground and comes back stronger than ever.

7. The Fact-Film

THE IDEA: SEARCH AND RESEARCH
SHAPING THE IDEA
THINKING ON FILM

A MOTION picture cannot be judged by filing items pro and con under a given number of headings. But headings, artificial though they be, are useful for purposes of study. They give form to a problem that is sprawling and full of intangibles. With this warning in mind, I list twelve headings under which you might consider a fact-film—Idea, Research, Organization, Framework, Beginning, Middle, Climax, End, Transitions, Dialogue, Narration and Characters. Practically everything said here about fact-films can be said of fictional films too.

THE IDEA: SEARCH AND RESEARCH

As for idea, the first question is, Was the idea worth the effort? And the money? Motion picture production under any circumstance is problem-prone and somewhat costly. A survey made by Eastman Kodak shows that the median cost of non-theatrical films is about $1,167 a screen minute. This is a pittance compared with the cost of theatrical films; it is difficult to make one of those for less than $10,000 a screen minute. As for high budget pictures, *Ben-Hur* cost more than $60,000 a screen minute, and the producer of *The Ten Commandments* said that the picture cost him more than a million dollars a commandment. It was not worth it artistically, but it was financially, for it has returned about five million dollars a commandment.

A weak idea costs the producer as much money and effort to develop as a strong idea. Sometimes a weak idea costs more money to develop than a good one because there is a tendency to try to cover flaws with production frills. There is no sadder sight than a threadbare idea dressed in a super-production—like an old crone outfitted by a distinguished couturier. A strong, fresh idea might carry a picture even if production slips below par. There are pictures, technically impeccable, that rock the audience in the cradle of ennui because they are a parade of clichés from fade-in to fade-out. But then there are the pictures that leave camera work and sound with much to be desired, but that hold the audience because they have fresh ideas wonderfully developed.

It is not enough for the idea to be fresh; it ought also to *need* the motion picture medium. It ought to demand to be *visual* and demand to be *in motion*. If it is an idea that demands sound only, maybe it should have been recorded on magnetic tape. Or if it needs visualization but not motion maybe it ought to have been a film strip. Sometimes an idea that could be made filmic is not conceived that way and ends up with what is really nothing more than a series of still pictures with sound track added.

As for research, there is a danger that someone writing a fact-film will go off half-cocked. So the next question to ask yourself is whether the writer knew his subject well enough to tell about it in a simple, clear, well-organized way. A script writer is often dealing with subjects he knows little or nothing about, but he makes up for this deficiency through detailed research—reading books and articles, and interviewing experts in the field.

An idea of what I mean by detailed research can be got from a series of case histories published by *The Saturday Evening Post*. *The Post* took some of its articles and showed step-by-step the time and effort that went into them. Since the non-fiction script writer must put himself through the same research discipline as the magazine article writer—a non-fiction film is really a magazine article in motion—let's take a brief look at one of the case histories, the one called *Opera's Funny Man,* by Maurice Zolotow.

When Zolotow decided to write about Salvatore Baccaloni, the basso buffo of the Metropolitan Opera, he set out on a program of research that would have discouraged a less professional writer. First, he read all the publicity the Met had on Baccaloni. Next, he read everything about the singer in the files of the New York *Times,* especially the reviews of the operas in which he had sung. Zolotow feared he did not know enough about opera to talk intelligently to the singer, so he read eight books on the subject. During this orientation period he hung around backstage at the Met to get the feel of the place. When he felt ready for Baccaloni, he interviewed the singer six times. He also interviewed ten of Baccaloni's friends.

Zolotow said, "About 80% of the research material is never used. Nevertheless, even the unused material gives the article depth." When a script writer does a shallow research job, he needs to use all the material gathered and the finished product shows it. There is something sleazy about the film and here and there a part is so thin the audience can see through it.

Between research and writing comes the discipline of organizing the material. The script writer may be so itchy to get writing that he will be tempted to let organization shift for itself. He does this at the peril of spawning a malformed script, one that forever wanders and never makes a telling point.

So notice if the script is built, like a good essay, out of major blocks of material, like-things grouped with like-things. If a documentary is about life in a native village, there will probably be a block about recreation, one about religion, one about food and one about work habits. Unless this material has been blocked out beforehand the chances are that religion will get entangled with recreation and the food get mixed up with the work habits. It is possible that religion and recreation will have overlapping parts, but those overlapping parts should be used as the transition scenes moving from the block about religion to the block about recreation.

In rare instances good documentaries are made without a script. It is a case of shoot and shoot and shoot and then sit down at the editing table and edit like-things with like-things. Flaherty used this system and made it work because he was willing to spend several years shooting a film.

Every film, like every piece of writing, has the problem of transition. Visually this is usually done with a dissolve. At the same time the narrator may say something that helps the audience make a smooth mental shift from one part of the film to the next without feeling jolted or lost.

SHAPING THE IDEA

Framework is something more easily described than defined. If ten excellent script writers were each given the same set of facts and asked to write a script, each would probably turn up with a different framework. The frameworks would differ, but not the facts. The framework is what the facts are hung on.

A writer was assigned to do a radio script using some statistics published by the National Safety Council. The statistics told about the number of deaths expected over a long holiday weekend. With the statistics there was some detail about the most frequent causes of those deaths. The writer needed a framework to hang the facts on. He decided to do a dramatization using Death as narrator. During the play, Death interrupts his talk with the audience to take a ride with several drivers who are violating laws mentioned in the statistics. If those statistics had been handed to ten writers each would have had to hew to the same facts, but each would have dreamed up a different framework to hang them on, some would have been good, some not so good. So here is a key point in judging a fact-film: How fresh was the idea for the framework? How appropriate? How effective?

To draw on one of Aristotle's ideas again: a work of art needs a beginning, a middle and an end. Since documentaries have their roots in the arts, they too need a beginning, a middle and an end.

The problem of the beginning is to get attention in the *right* way. That word *right* is so important. Anybody can get attention in the wrong way. Edith Wharton has told of an English schoolboy who tried his hand at short story writing, and, with pencil poised, recalled hearing that the beginning of a short story should catch attention. So he wrote, " 'Damn,' said the Duchess as she lit her cigar." But nothing after that sentence could match it. Could the boy have sustained the interest stirred up by that sentence, he would, Miss Wharton thought, have had one of the great short stories of all time.

The danger is that the beginning will be one of two extremes —too full of shock treatment or too pedestrian. The beginning must be in harmony with what follows; it should press a button that throws a light down the rest of the script.

Banquet speakers have abused more beginnings than it is well to dwell on. They have an icky way of starting with a joke that has nothing to do with the speech that follows. Even if the joke is good, and it rarely is, it ought not be used unless it throws some light on the speech. A joke followed by an unrelated speech is as aesthetically unsightly as a papier mâché mask on a human body. In telling the joke the speaker keeps part of the rule for beginnings, he gets attention, maybe, but he does not get attention in the *right* way. Film-makers are as faulty as speech makers when they open with a BIG beginning; so often it is an atomic explosion followed by humble subject matter.

How long should a beginning be? How deep is a well? The beginning should be in proportion to the body of the film the way an animal's head is in proportion to its body. (Here is

Aristotle again, if I am not mistaken.) The usual danger is that the beginning is too large, something of a cow's head on a goat's body. The too-much beginning is a common excess in all forms of writing. So many beginnings reveal a writer just flexing his muscles, warming-up. For this reason all beginnings should be viewed through the narrowed eyes of suspicion.

The middle of the film is everything that falls between the end of the beginning to the beginning of the end. Here the information is given in large blocks of material with transitions leading from one block to another. The middle must have unity. It gets unity by having a dominant theme. The theme has to do with the spirit of the picture; it is something the picture is saturated with, something the picture exudes. At least that is what I mean by the word. *Marty* was saturated with loneliness; *High Noon* was shot through with duty; *Turn of the Screw* exuded a mysterious evil. The fact-film about holiday accidents had a theme of danger. A picture promoting a certain make of tractor might have as its theme robustness. The theme should be in every frame of the finished film.

If the writer is conscientious in his research, he will uncover many bits of information that are interesting but that do not fit into his theme. He needs the courage to throw them away, or to save them for another film. The writer dare not sacrifice the unity that a dominant theme gives, for if he does he will blur the communication and will leave the audience hazy about the information he wants it to retain.

The climax comes just before the end of the picture. It is a level slightly higher than any reached in the course of the film. The climax is a necessity in the fictional film; that is where we get the flight across the rooftops, the brawl in the barroom, the shoot-out in the middle of the street—something that resolves the conflicts, or at least eases them momentarily. In non-fiction films also reaching a high point just before the end is good technique. Even if the picture is about such a prosaic thing as a demonstration of how bird seed is packaged, it can reach a higher point by showing a quick review of all the steps that were described in detail earlier in the film. The ending has but one assignment, to let you, the audience, out gracefully. It must have the "feel" of ending and there is not much more that can be said about it. What do I mean by "feel"? If someone played a phonograph record you had never heard, you would know when the ending was coming without looking at the record, you would know by the feel of it. And so with a film: there must be an inevitableness and a rightness about the ending. The audience must sense that here is a good place to get off.

THINKING ON FILM

As for dialogue, the question is: Does it have the ring of conversation? The tendency is to make dialogue too heavy, to have people making speeches at each other rather than conversing. Sometimes it is too stilted. Spoken sentences are usually shorter than those written to be read. Spoken sentences are often fragmentary, and filled with contractions and with references to the second person and the first person. Spoken sentences usually have more carefree rhetoric than those written to be read. The test is: does it have the *ring* of conversation, not is it *like* conversation? Dialogue that is a transcript of real conversation is dreary business, indeed. Real conversations are much too rambling and undisciplined for good dialogue. Dialogue must get up and go some place while making the audience believe that this is really the way conversation sounds.

Non-fictional films do not have as much of a problem with dialogue as do fictional, simply because there is less of it. Usually a non-fictional film is shot silent. Narration, music and sound effects are added to the sound track later.

Of all the things that can be wrong with a non-theatrical

film the chances are the wrongness will be in the narration more often than any place else. The sound track is often too loaded, too full of talk. The script should be written to tell the story as visually as possible; the narrator should be used only to tell those things that cannot be known visually.

In the excellent documentary, *The City,* there is a sequence that shows a haunted little man frustrated by the signs of the world: *Stop, Go, Keep off the Grass, No Parking, Don't Cross Here.* He ducks and cringes beneath the signs until we begin to laugh, but in the laughter there is sympathy for the man caged by the don'ts of life. If a narrator had kept interrupting, "Look out, Joe, they got you coming and going. You turn to the right and there is one. To the left, oops, there's another! Where will it all end?" the sequence would have been spoiled. It only lasted about thirty seconds but it is a powerful editorial about man-made complexities. It is the most powerful type of editorial because it is one that plants an idea in the viewer's mind and gives him enough facts so that he writes the editorial in his thoughts. The editorial he writes is the one he believes in most; he feels it is his own idea. It is much more effective than one foisted onto him full-blown.

There is supposed to be a psychological principle that at a given instant one can only look intently or listen intently. If this is true, then in a documentary when the visual is important the narration should be held down, and when the narrator is making an important point the screen should not be too active. I recall a sequence that featured bombs bursting and soldiers charging and everything else that could make the screen jump with activity, and all through it the narrator rattled away until, I feel sure, at the close of the sequence no one knew a word he had said.

Tone is another problem of narration. The tendency, as always, is to swing to extremes—too pompous or too cute. Good taste—which someone defined as proper dignity—would require that narration be kept from either extreme.

The spirit of the narrator is so important. Often he is selected for his voice, but that is all he has, and the audience senses that here is shallowness with voice added. The narrator is so taken with forming pear-shaped tones and with listening to the melody of his own voice that he is not really interested in communicating information. Just sounds. Two of the best narrators I have heard on sound tracks were non-professionals. One was an old artist who explained what he found of interest in color, textures and design around a deserted farm. The other, also an artist, explained a painting step-by-step from rough sketch to finished canvas. In each instance the audience sensed it listened to a man who wanted very much to communicate ideas and information. Both artists felt every sentence, and both lacked concern for mellifluous tones. They put first things first and so their narration had a sincerity and an honesty sometimes lacking in professionals.

Characters in a documentary, even minor ones, need to have blood in their veins. The non-fiction film usually exists to give information and not to show character development, but the people in it should not be mere shadows flitting across a screen. The characters in the Flaherty documentaries, *Man of Aran,* and *Louisiana Story,* are as carefully drawn as they are in a work of fiction.

Minor characters are given individuality through little touches. In *The City,* a Negro returns to his home in the slums and just before he walks up on the front porch he shoos a chicken from the steps, a detail that makes him and his neighborhood stick in the mind. Also in *The City,* a man stands up to talk in a town meeting and his wife's hand reaches out to tug at his coat-tail. Another little touch in the same picture is the brief blacksmith shop sequence. An old loafer sitting near the forge leans back every time a shower of sparks spray toward him; he is too lazy to get up and move. The Negro, the town hall speaker, the loafer, each has only five or six seconds on the screen, yet each sticks in the mind because the little touch told something about him.

So much for standards of the non-theatrical film. It is easy to see that the non-theatrical and the theatrical motion picture have things in common, for both aim to impart—idea, information, emotion.

8. The Impact of Television

GUIDES TO GOOD VIEWING
BABY SITTER OR EDUCATOR?

SURVEYS show that thirty-three percent of the television set owners flip a knob and accept whatever comes shimmering into view. The system is as unreasonable as walking blindfold into a library, groping toward the shelves and checking out the first book that comes to hand. Anyone who accepts television on a catch-as-catch-can basis is certain to waste time. The percentages are against him, for the inane programs outnumber the substantial.

Television can be of real value if used with sense and reason. As I said in the early pages, some things on television can help us feel the texture of life—*Requiem for a Heavyweight, Call Me Back* and *Catered Affair*. Television lets us live beyond what our own living can be—*Project 20, Twentieth Century* and *John Gunther's High Road*. It informs through newscasts, panel discussions and special events telecasts. It teaches with *Camera Three, Continental Classroom* and the lectures of Leonard Bernstein.

Most shows on television are for entertainment only. The audience has the problem of finding the ones that entertain at a certain altitude, such as the specials *Peter Pan, Annie Get Your Gun* and *An Evening with Fred Astaire*.

Television takes its cue from popular taste. What people watch on television is not just the individual's problem but part of a national problem, for what is followed and what is shunned shapes this powerful medium. And it is powerful. A Roper poll learned what a grip TV has when it asked: "Suppose you could continue to have only one of the following—

radio, television, newspapers or magazines—which one of the four would you want to keep?" To that question, forty-two percent answered that they would keep television, thirty-two percent newspapers, nineteen percent radio, four percent magazines, and three percent did not know.

GUIDES TO GOOD VIEWING

This powerful influence on the national culture is doomed to emptiness if the audience supports the inane. To show how the impression gets around that the audience prefers inanities, the producers of *Playhouse 90* will tell you that the only time their program was rated among the ten most popular shows was the week they dropped drama in favor of Mike Todd's Madison Square Garden party. When an inferior show is supported that is unfortunate, but when something superior is allowed to die from inattention, that is tragic. Some programs that would be nice to have around have died for lack of attention: *See It Now, The Search, American Inventory, Odyssey, Seven Lively Arts, Studio One, Mr. Peepers, You Are There, Goodyear-Philco Television Playhouse, What in the World?* and *Wide Wide World.* The list of such happy memories could be extended.

How is one to know what TV programs are worthy of attention? It takes a little doing to find out. The critics can help. At least they can lead you toward, or head you off from, a regular series. But what about the specials—those things that are here tonight and gone forever; a review of them in tomorrow's paper is not much help.

For specials you will have to make a judgment in advance. To do that you will have to keep up on television news. The log in the daily paper is not helpful, since it does not give details. *TV Guide* is useful because it runs a box giving details about programs above run-of-the-mill. The back page of *Time* lists shows that give promise for the week to come. Some newspapers run weekly TV supplements that include news articles about major programs scheduled for the week.

If you want to get the most from television you ought to get in the habit of following the credits. They will make you familiar with the names of people who have the habit of doing things well. If the program you watched was not worth watching, the credits will not be worth watching either, but if you see something that is more than lackluster, note the name of the director and the producer. You will find that certain directors tend to get the best shows, because they can do the most with what they get, and certain producers have a way of organizing things with a little distinction to them. After you have made such observations, when you see a familiar name in a preview article it will prompt you to watch the program.

As a start, here are some directors worth following: Robert Mulligan, Delbert Mann, John Frankenheimer, George Schaefer, Franklin Schaffner, Tom Donovan and Alan Schneider.

Here are some producers that have brought good things to the television screen: Robert Saudek, Robert Herridge, Martin Manulis, Fred Coe, John Houseman, Herbert Brodkin, Robert Graff, Mildred Freed Alberg, David Susskind, Gordon Duff, Robert Alan Arthur, Richard Walsh, Pamela Ilott, Arthur Penn, Burton Benjamin, Fred Friendly, Edward R. Murrow.

There is no point of talking about programs worthy of the power of television without giving specific examples. Here are some programs on the air in the Spring of 1960 that are examples of television well used: *Camera Three, World Wide 60, John Gunther's High Road, American Scene, Lamp Unto My Feet, Look Up and Live, Johns Hopkins File, College News Conference, Ask Washington, Open Hearing, Conquest, G.E. College Bowl, Time: Present, Small World, Meet the Press, Twentieth Century, Our American Heritage, Woman!, Du-Pont Show of the Month, General Electric Theater, Ford Startime, Hallmark Hall of Fame, Project 20, Wisdom, Sunday*

Showcase, Playhouse 90, Continental Classroom, U.S. Steel Hour, Pontiac Star Parade, Bell Telephone Hour, NBC Opera, CBS Reports.

I missed some good ones, I am sure; for one thing I omitted the specials that do not fit into a regular series, and I did not attempt to survey programs beamed by the fifty educational stations, and I made no effort to track down excellent local shows that are little known outside their areas. But the list is complete enough to give you an idea of what I mean by television worthy of your time. Certainly, I have listed more programs than anyone has time to watch.

BABY SITTER OR EDUCATOR?

I kept children's shows off the list because I want to talk about them separately. The effect of television on children causes more concern than anything else about the medium. The concern is not unfounded, because, as Plato said, children should be guided by a love of excellence even in play. There is much on television that does not guide by a love of excellence.

George Santayana said, "In poetry, feeling is transferred by contagion . . ." In all the arts and in all forms of communication there is a certain "catching" of attitudes, especially in the young. To put it bluntly, everyone who appears on the TV screen is a "carrier." The attitudes that Superman and Sheena infect children with are not those that lead to a love of excellence.

The channels are not crowded with children's shows that lead to a love of excellence. Among the good ones are *Captain Kangaroo, Mr. Wizard, Disneyland, Ding Dong School, Romper Room, Huckleberry Hound* and *Young People's Concerts.* It is too bad we lost *Kukla, Fran and Ollie, Zoo Parade, The Boing-Boing Show* and *Let's Take a Trip,* for we could use them.

In any discussion about the effect television has on children the tendency is to go whooping off to one extreme or the other. I tend toward one extreme and I and my fellow extremists are a lonely lot; most of the extremists are at the other end of the pasture.

I am of the extreme that gives television more credit than it deserves. Whenever children show knowledge that surprises me I tend to give credit to TV, a credit sometimes misplaced. I was reminded of that while reading an essay by Coventry Patmore written before the coming of TV. In writing about children's intuitive knowledge, Patmore tells of a seven-year-old boy saying, "What makes this ball drop when I leave hold of it?—Oh, I know, the ground pulls it." The child had never heard of the Newtonian theory of gravitation. Patmore tells of another child, who while stretching out on a gravel path staring intently at pebbles, said, "They are alive. They are always wanting to burst, but something draws them in."

If the essay had been written since the coming of television I would have suspected that the children had been watching Don Herbert's *Mr. Wizard* or Dr. Harvey White's *Continental Classroom*.

The other extremists give TV more discredit than it deserves. They fear it will develop a generation of monsters all eyes and no brains. Some of the things I have read lead me to think that their side is as wrong as mine. Here are some examples:

"For years teachers, principals, superintendents, and school boards everywhere have been wearied by the cry of businessmen—'The boys you send us can't spell!' "

Is that familiar? It sounds like something from today's newspaper or from a current magazine. It happens to be taken from Warren Hicks' *Champion Spelling Book*, printed in 1909.

"The children now love luxury; they have bad manners and contempt for authority; they show disrespect for elders and love chatter in place of exercise. Children are tyrants, not the servants of their household. They no longer rise when elders enter the room. They contradict their parents, chatter before company, gobble up dainties at the table, cross their legs and tyrannize their teachers."

Socrates said that twenty-five centuries before TV.

"Our earth is degenerated in these latter days, there are signs that the world is speedily coming to an end; bribery and corruption are common; children no longer obey their parents. . . ."

Those are chippings on an Assyrian Stone Tablet of 2800 B.C.

I do not know what parents blamed the shortcomings of the children on before the coming of TV. I suppose the wife said to the husband, "Look at the little monster—just like your family," and maybe he said, "I thought he took after you." Now both parents can point to the TV set and say, "That did it!" An electronic scapegoat is a convenient thing to have around the house.

There is something to be said on both sides: for the few of us who give credit to TV and for the sizeable group that discredits it. Both sides can find things to point to in the findings of the study made by the Queensboro, Long Island, Public Library. The study shows that when TV is new in a community the circulation figures at the library go down like a toboggan. But when the novelty has worn off—it takes about two years —circulation figures begin to climb and in some instances surpass all previous circulation records. This circulation boom, some believe, comes about because television gives readers new interests.

The problem that confronts children when faced with a television set is the same as that which confronts adults: How to use the thing within sense and reason? If someone asks me how to get children to use it properly I dodge the question by saying that the answer is filed under D for discipline, and not under A for aesthetics. It may be difficult enough for parents to discipline themselves as far as TV is concerned without taking on the burden of child discipline, too. But I just don't know an easier answer.

You can read the critics, and follow the credits on the screen, and keep posted on what magazines predict will be programs worth watching, but when all is said and done it is possible that somebody's educated guess went haywire and what you find on the screen is not worth your time. At that point there is one simple rule to remember: the knob that turns on the set is the same one that turns it off. As Ernie Kovacs said, "Science has given us hands with which to turn off television sets."

9. The Electronic Classroom

TEACHING: LIVE OR TELEVISED?
THE TELEVISED TEACHER
EDUCATIONAL PROGRAMING
ANNEX TO THE SCHOOL

It is a rare child who enters first grade this year not having had at least a glimpse of ballet, an opera, a rodeo, a political gathering, a World Series game, a Shakespearean play. These things have been shimmering on television screens for as long as today's children can remember. The great-grandfathers of most of these children grew old and died without seeing one such event.

By the time the children have finished the eighth grade they will have witnessed more major events than any man who lived out his life before the coming of television. Does so much direct experience get in the way of perceiving and thinking? Does too much consuming dull the creative edge? Do today's children with their greater storehouse of experience learn more readily than did their parents? Are children's minds so coated with shallow sophistication that teachers find it impossible to chip through?

I have no one-sentence answer for those questions, but in a few dozen pages I might be able to give some idea of how I feel about television as a teaching medium.

TEACHING: LIVE OR TELEVISED?

One thing is certain: television does teach. For good or for evil it does teach, adults as well as children, but especially children. They are being taught during every waking hour, no matter what; they bristle with thousands of little antennae that vibrate all the time. Television, like everything else they experience, either elevates their standards or debases them, but it does not leave them alone.

If television is such a powerful cultural influence, the most powerful of our time, then teachers had better get together with it. Even teachers who use the word television with a shudder should make an uneasy truce with it. Such teachers might find consolation in knowing that some people looked down on the printing press when it was invented, fearing that it meant the lowering of culture, and others belittled the blackboard when it was introduced into the classroom, predicting the end of sound teaching practices. But time has not proven that printed books and classroom blackboards have caused an impoverishment of culture.

In accepting an honorary degree from the University of Notre Dame, General David Sarnoff stated: "In your Convocation Program, I note Father Hesburgh's statement that 'a university can no more ignore television today than universities of the past could have ignored the discovery of printing.' I am impressed with the cogency and aptness of this comparison. We are too prone to make technological instruments the scapegoats for the sins of those who wield them. The products of modern science are not in themselves good or bad; it is the way they are used that determines their value.

"Admittedly the advent of printing made possible the spread of a great deal of mediocre, trashy and detrimental writings. But it also made possible the vast dissemination of the Bible, the thoughts of great seers and philosophers, the accumulated literary treasures of our civilization. On balance, few will doubt that man has been enriched and ennobled by Herr Gutenberg's invention. And the same holds true for Marconi's invention."

The argument about whether or not teaching via TV can be effective has died down of late. The Very Rev. C. J. Steiner, S. J., president of the University of Detroit, said, "Television instruction is no longer a matter of debate. It has been proven and accepted that television students are on a par with those under traditional teaching. Television is not a gimmick. It is a useful teaching tool."

Father Steiner hopes that television will help this country out of its gigantic educational problem. He points out that colleges and universities are being prepared for a 1970 enrollment of six million. Yet today plant facilities and faculties are straining to handle half that number.

Father Steiner does not see TV as a mere emergency measure to be used only as long as there is an educational housing shortage. He believes TV teaching can join classroom teaching to make a real contribution. Other teachers at Detroit who have tried television teaching feel the same way. I heard one of them give an enthusiastic report on his experiences in teaching Spanish on television. He admits he started the year filled with foreboding but ended it pleased with the new medium.

Another member of the Detroit faculty, Father Herman J. Mueller, S. J., found teaching history on television a stimulating, and backbreaking, experience. Father Mueller was teaching in classrooms twenty-two years before he tried teaching in the little electronics schoolhouse. He believes he can cover as much material in thirty minutes on TV as he used to cover in a fifty-minute classroom session. He feels his lectures are freshened by the need to make each a compact unit, with no loose ends dangling. To make sure that the lecture is compact and that the timing is right, he spends three and a half hours preparing the outline that he and the director use. He no longer uses the blackboard because writing takes up precious time, so he carefully prepares charts to illustrate key points. A TV professor, he says, even roots out such time-stalling phrases as, "Now by that I mean . . ."

Everybody has experienced the rambling teacher and anything that disciplines him gets my applause. In Latin I had one who was a baseball fan. We often detoured him into baseball; for us a living game held more fascination than a dead language. In philosophy, the teacher evidently could not recognize a goof when he saw one. One student was a 33rd degree goof who knew the password and the secret handshake; he was always bringing up some asinine question that started, "But supposing . . ." The teacher honored each question as though it had been posed by Thomas Aquinas and wasted the semester for the rest of the class.

These are the things people forget who argue against TV teaching. They continue to talk as though each classroom enshrines an ideal situation. I admit that television can never be a substitute for the great teacher with a few students gathered around, but great teachers with few students are getting as rare as Mark Hopkinses sitting on the ends of logs. With the growing student population, the only way a great teacher can reach a goodly percentage of the student body is through some form of television.

THE TELEVISED TEACHER

For television is just a means of transportation, a way of getting a teacher around to more students; there is no substitute for an excellent teacher face to face with a few students.

What is an excellent teacher? A safe conclusion is that an excellent teacher does not necessarily know more about the subject than the mediocre teacher; he might even know less about it. The distinguishing mark of an excellent teacher is that he makes a student care. He makes the material come to life. He makes it exciting, stimulating, clear. He projects himself and his material into his class. He may give quite a show, but he does not need to; he can be quiet and calm and still send the subject matter singing home.

The excellent teacher has a "sense of audience." He is forever asking himself, if not consciously at least subconsciously: What do they know about this? What do they care about it? How can they be made to care? Can they grasp it if it is presented in this way? In other words he is always teaching for the sake of the student. Not for the sake of self-expression, not even for the sake of the subject, but for the sake of the student.

Teaching is an art. Only because I believe that teaching is an art, and can be practiced via television, have I included this chapter.

In his book, *The Art of Teaching,* Gilbert Highet says: "When the pupils come to you their minds are only half-formed, full of blank spaces and vague notions and over-simplifications. You do not merely insert a lot of facts, if you teach them properly. It is not like injecting 500 cc. of serum, or administering a year's dose of vitamins.

"You take the living mind and mould it . . . often it comes into firmer shape as you work, and gives you the incomparable happiness of helping to create a human being.

"To teach a boy the difference between truth and lies in print, to start him thinking about the meanings of poetry or patriotism . . . gives the sort of satisfaction that an artist has when he makes a picture out of blank canvas and chemical colorings. . . ."

A poor classroom teacher will be a poor television teacher, and a good classroom teacher will probably be a good television teacher. But the good classroom teacher will be effective on television only if he is adaptable enough to change his methods to fit the new medium.

If a teacher is going to teach successfully by closed-circuit, or regular television, he needs the willingness to try the untried. He must have some sense of adventure, and cannot be a person immobilized by a concern for his own security and softness of life. He needs courage and self-confidence to teach a course knowing that his colleagues are monitoring it. He must be able to work with others, for all television production, even at its simplest, is a teamwork affair. If he has flair, that is fine, but it is not absolutely necessary.

Closed-circuit teaching has had favorable acceptance in schools that have tried it. In the beginning there is a tendency for teachers to be against it, perhaps because the word *television* is involved. The very word causes all kinds of alarm bells to clang inside them; it brings to mind quiz shows, gun fights and soap opera. If they could forget the word and think of television as a mechanical device that helps a teacher reach more students, many of their early fears might be quieted.

To get outstanding teachers around to more students, there may some day be syndicated teachers the way we now have syndicated writers. On any given morning, Littleburg College in the Midwest might present, via closed-circuit, a lecture on Shakespeare from the University of Southern California, semantics from the University of Chicago, foreign affairs from Georgetown and history from Harvard.

This sounds like a college built around a switchboard instead of a faculty, that is a college president's dream, a catalogue full of courses and not a complaining faculty member on the campus. Maybe there would be on campus a few teaching machines, and in time no doubt they would learn to complain.

I think that closed-circuit, and teacher syndicates, and teaching machines and some things as yet undreamed of can be used to help educate the young. Many of these things will be misused, for man's frayed edge of fallibility will always show. Not even electronics can insure against that.

Some teachers see TV as a form of automation dedicated to making them unwanted. So far, whenever closed-circuit was used properly it did not eliminate teachers; it merely re-deployed them. I admit there is a danger that administrators may try to use TV as a money-saving device and go too far in eliminating face-to-face teaching. Of the many systems of closed-circuit teaching tried the one that seems to work best is to have a classroom teacher orient the class for the TV lecture, monitor the lecture with the class and lead a discussion afterward. Incidentally, the attitude of this classroom teacher is a big factor in the success or failure of a TV course. If the classroom teacher is unwilling to give the new system a trial, he communicates his suspicions to the students, and this has a bearing on their acceptance of TV instruction.

There is still a great deal to learn about how to teach effectively with television. Studies so far indicate that most subjects can be taught about as well on television as in the classroom. Some things can be taught better on television— rote learning subjects and those that require detailed demonstrations.

Studies show that students in the bottom third of the class are the ones that get the most value from closed-circuit teaching. Perhaps that is because the teacher constructs his class presentation more thoroughly and spells out things more carefully. The top third learn well no matter if the instructor meets them face to face or comes to them over television.

A member of the American Medical Association told me with enthusiasm how a TV camera can peer into a microscope and enlarge a cell to 980 times its size so that a professor can point out its various parts to a class. A member of the American Dental Association praised television as a teaching aid. A camera staring into a patient's mouth shows more students more clearly how things look the instant a hot drill hits a live nerve. All the medics agree that their television must be in color; black and white is not too useful for them.

But can abstract ideas be taught by television?

Stephens College for women at Columbia, Missouri, experimented with teaching the abstract over closed-circuit. Stephens introduced an ideas course and required that all beginning students, nearly a thousand, take it. The college installed a closed-circuit system with fifty-two viewing sets, one set for about every eighteen girls.

The next problem was to find a man capable of putting abstract ideas in an interesting, exciting, graspable way. Stephens found him in Reuel Denney, of the University of Chicago. Starting at eleven o'clock two mornings a week, Mr. Denney lectured over closed-circuit for twenty minutes. Then in each of the fifty-two viewing rooms a teacher led the girls in a forty-minute discussion. This was followed by lunch at which girls and teachers continued the discussion. Stephens was pleased with the results.

I said earlier that there is no substitute for an excellent teacher face to face with a small group of students. But what about the excellent teacher face to face with a vast audience? With college populations growing, the vast audience will be more usual than the intimate group. Perhaps it would be better for the student to get the lecture from a television screen instead of as part of a vast class. At least an experiment conducted at Penn State seems to indicate that.

A group of students were assigned seats in a large auditorium. After a few days of lectures the students were told that closed-circuit television sets were available to them in other parts of the building and that they might have a few days to try out both the face-to-face lecture and the TV lecture. After several days the students were told they would have to make up their minds which they want to attend for the rest of the semester—face-to-face or TV screen. The students who sat near the lecturer stayed in the auditorium. Half way back in the auditorium some went and some stayed. In the back of the auditorium practically everybody went to the monitors.

EDUCATIONAL PROGRAMING

Everything said about closed-circuit so far can be said about teaching via an educational station. There are fifty stations devoted to education only—no commercials, no give-away shows, no situation comedies—only education. Since they do not stress entertainment and are not permitted to accept money from advertisers, they wear a lean and hungry look. At best, theirs is a life of shabby gentility. Some are financed by community subscription, some are university owned, and some are financed by the state.

Partly because of a gaunt budget, educational stations have been guilty of some lackluster programing. They try to log too much air time; educational stations telecast on the average of twenty-five hours a week, with some doing as much as fifty hours. If only they would all make it a policy of filling just as much time as they can fill well, and not trouble the air with material simply because the station is there!

Then too, the educational stations are still in the process of developing a new breed of man—the educational producer, or director. In speaking of the need for this new breed, Dr. Huston Smith, of M.I.T., said, "If educational television is to realize its potential, it must attract and hold creative talent of the first magnitude. I am not talking about teachers. I am talking about producers and directors. For those are the forgotten—or rather unconceived—men in educational television today."

Professor Smith, who has done quite a bit of teaching by television, laments the fact that when educators start talking about television they never talk about securing really outstanding producers and directors. "Somehow the idea is abroad that all that is needed for good educational television is a good teacher. Take a man who knows his stuff, who is sincere and articulate, and who can 'make contact,' put him before a camera and the result is likely to be good television teaching. This seems to be the prevailing assumption. It is not true.

"Nothing in drama can take the place of great acting, but a great actor is not enough to insure a great play. We have come to recognize great directing as an art in its own right, indispensable in eliciting the full talents of those on the stage. The need for great directing in educational television is no less."

This new breed should be well-educated men with a feel for television. They need sense and taste and tact. The tact is useful when they have to improve the instruction of some teachers without arousing too much resentment. Imagine the problem they will have if they get a teacher who speaks the way a university president spoke at a meeting of educators:

"The effectiveness of the teacher in broadcasting would be unimportant without another element in the new exploration, also one not within the interests of commercial television and radio. I refer to the large numbers of people who are eager for serious learning experience and who are eager to undertake systematic study with the help of the teacher-broadcaster."

Did you understand that paragraph after one reading? Certainly, you could not have grasped it after one listening. It is so filled with sound that the sense is drowned out. Such talk crowds many a teachers' conference. The only way an educational director can help a teacher who talks that way is to rip out the old icky spirit and plug in a new, clean-cut spirit that loves simplicity and directness. Or is that impossible?

A big boost to educational television came with the establishment of the Educational Television and Radio Center, financed by the Ford Foundation. The center provides films and kinescopes to educational stations. It gets much of its best material by footing the bill for programs produced for it and by dipping into the foreign market.

Another help to educational stations has been an NBC experiment started three years ago. It began producing programs especially for educational stations. This indicates that commercial stations and educational stations are on friendly terms, although that could not have been foreseen a few years ago when the FCC set aside 242 channels for educational use and the commercial men howled like bitter banshees.

Perhaps the unselfish attitude of educational stations has helped. For example, the executive director of WTTW, Chicago's educational station, said, "If we develop an educational program that draws a large following, and if a commercial station wants to take it over and sell it to a sponsor, I'll say go ahead. It isn't important who transmits the program; the important thing is that educational programs be available."

Another reason commercial stations can look with kindliness on educational stations is that the educators are not exactly cornering the TV audience. The executive director of WTTW said that surveys indicate that some of the stations' programs reach an audience of only 15,000. He said that almost with apology, but he need not apologize. While 15,000 does not sound like many when compared with the numbers Ed Sullivan must draw in the Chicago area, yet 15,000 students make a sizeable university. It is important in these days of crowded schools that 15,000 persons can learn something without occupying an inch of classroom space. And when a teacher reaches 15,000 by television he is reaching more than he will reach in a lifetime of classroom teaching.

NBC began its experiment in the spring of 1957 by sending out educational programs late each afternoon to the educational TV stations. The experiment was so successful that NBC has been doing educational programing ever since.

In 1958, NBC started an early morning course in atomic physics and revived an American custom long dormant, the custom of rising before dawn to study. Van Wyck Brooks in *The Flowering of New England* tells us that a hundred years ago many citizens of Boston, Cambridge and Concord arose before dawn for self-improvement. Daybreak found scholars of all ages and of all walks of life grappling with Greek, pondering Plato and scanning sonnets. It was not unusual for young ladies to arise at four o'clock to read some of *Paradise Lost* to set the tone for the day. The more serious minded read from the *Bhagavad-Gita,* contemplating the world's potentialities rather than its actualities.

Each week-day morning all over the United States several hundred thousand people are getting up before dawn to study, thanks to NBC. I suppose NBC and its affiliated commercial stations had the courage to present a physics course at 6:30 a.m. because of the success a New York station had with its *Sunrise Semester* series in literature.

What an enthusiastic reception the pre-dawn physics course got! A mother in Detroit wrote, "This is the only educational program I can watch undisturbed by my three monsters." A high school sophomore in Naperville, Illinois, had long caused his parents concern with his late rising, but when he got interested in the physics course, he set the alarm for six o'clock and awakened the whole family. He continued causing concern but in a different way. In Greenwich, Connecticut, police spotted a fifteen-year-old boy on the street before 6 a.m. When he told them he was on his way to school they took him to an all-night diner to phone his parents, but found there the boy's physics teacher drinking coffee. The teacher said he gathers with his students at school each morning to take the course on *Continental Classroom*.

NBC asked the 265 colleges and universities that had offered credits for the physics course what they would like next and they said a chemistry course. So for the 1959-'60 school year the chemistry course was taught at 6:30 a.m. and the physics course was rerun at 6 a.m.

Pulse, Inc., made a survey of teachers who had taken the physics course and found that 97.5 percent believed it had been of value to them. And 54.2 percent said that they had changed their teaching methods as a result of the course. This confirms a conclusion the Ford Foundation reached in studying teaching via television. The study said that when superior teachers are used on TV, the quality of teaching done by other teachers is upgraded, especially that of beginning teachers.

How explain this renaissance of rising before dawn's early light for self-improvement? NBC believes the desire, long dormant, was awakened in a dramatic way on October 4, 1957. An NBC report said that Sputnik made Americans realize that what was accomplished "could have been accomplished only by a nation having human resources, personnel in depth, fully trained in a wide range of scientific and technical fields."

Maybe this gave Americans an inferiority complex. The early morning study in New England was supposed to have something to do with a feeling of inferiority; the best intellects around Boston, Cambridge and Concord felt that their work was inferior to the literary work of England and the scholarship of Germany. Human beings have two high octane fuels—a feeling of inferiority and one of love.

Of all the ideas for educational television, the most dramatic so far is the plan to have an airplane circle Montpelier, Indiana, for six hours a day, four days a week starting in September, 1961. A video tape recorder inside it will send courses over a 200-mile radius. This academic umbrella will cover all of Indiana, and parts of Illinois, Kentucky, Michigan, Ohio and Wisconsin. Beneath it will sit five million students in 13,000 schools and colleges. Of the twenty-four courses offered during the first year, most will be for grade schools and high schools, with a few for colleges. Lectures in mathematics, foreign languages and the humanities will be throbbing in the air and anyone who wants them can have them for the price of a UHF television set. About seven million dollars is being spent to get this program, literally, off the ground. The money is coming from the Ford Foundation, from private gifts and from industrial grants. After it is well begun, the states involved are expected to finance it.

The group behind all this, called the Midwest Council for Airborne Television Instruction, lists several advantages of this system in prose that is not quite as facile as the flight of a plane. Of the advantages listed the only one that interests me is that the plane will stretch the reach of the ablest teachers. The kind of wonders that can be wrought by an exceptional teacher is told in an article in *America* (Oct. 31, 1959): "Sister Mary Lauretta, a science teacher at the little Catholic high school in Marshfield, Wisconsin, is unquestionably one of the world's greatest teachers. Every year for the past five years one of her students has been a winner in what is probably the nation's most difficult scholastic competition—the Westinghouse Science Talent Search. Such a record is roughly equal to hitting a home run in every game of the season, writing five best-selling novels, or swimming the Pacific, shore to shore. *Life* recently (April 6, 1959) published a three-page picture story about her teaching, describing it as 'dedicated,' 'inspiring,' 'energetic,' 'extraordinary.' Leading educators have expressed high praise for her classroom techniques. She has even received a commendation from President Eisenhower."

The only advantage of the flying classroom, as I see it, is to get the Sister Mary Laurettas of this world around to more students. If her course is taped and beamed throughout the Midwest she will reach more students in one semester than she can reach in dozens of lifetimes of classroom teaching.

ANNEX TO THE SCHOOL

Educational channels and closed-circuit systems are not the only ways television can help the learning process. A teacher can use regular commercial programing to help motivate classroom learning. I will start my defense for that last sentence by quoting from the book, *Crisis in Communication:*

"Today the more influential creative work is carried on by persons who instruct us without, generally, being aware that they are doing so. The person who is suspicious of the clergyman's intentions awaits without suspicion for the message of Ava Gardner, Jackie Gleason, Frank Sinatra and Marilyn Monroe."

These extra-curricular teachers and the classroom teachers are in competition. The classroom teacher is becoming more aware of it each year. Perhaps that is why I was asked to speak about motion pictures, television and radio at the conference of the National Catholic Education Association. Such a frivolous-sounding topic would not have been on the program a generation ago. But now teachers want to know who the extra-curricular teachers are and who among them can be helpful in education.

A few years ago, George E. Sokolsky, in his syndicated newspaper column, berated a teacher who admitted he relates homework assignments with radio and television programs. Mr. Sokolsky said, "I thought that we sent our children to school to learn how to read and write, how to do arithmetic, algebra, trigonometry, Latin, French, history, and similar subjects. Surely I do not send them to school to gain knowledge from *Cisco Kid, Martin Kane, Private Eye,* or *Crime Busters* or . . . Milton Berle or Sid Caesar!"

The teacher probably did not use any of the programs Mr. Sokolsky named. Programs cannot be grabbed at random; they must be selected with care to fit into the teaching plan. Only a teacher with sense and skill can use these things properly; otherwise the classroom turns into an arena for fun and games.

I can defend much of modern education with some grace because I am not a product of it. I even used a slate, that's how old-hat our teaching system was, and although the hickory stick was no longer considered an essential teaching tool, it was not wholly frowned upon. Education was more grim then, but not necessarily more glorious. It was akin to the soul-searing medicine of boyhood that went down like liquid mortal sin, but that was not nearly so effective as the more palatable medicines of today.

I admit that tying motion pictures and television into education is not easy. Useful programs are scant enough, but the teacher who works at it can find things that will help make classroom work come alive. A good teacher might even twist an uneducational program to suit her purposes; she realizes that as soon as a child becomes interested in television he leaves himself wide open for an education.

A teacher in Louisville knew her little buckaroos were

riding many dusty hours with TV cowhands. She knew that the cowboy on television resembles a real cowboy even less than Our Miss Brooks resembles a real teacher. Her class thought that cowboys are always kicking over tables and shooting out the lights, and that they keep their horses untied at the hitching post for a quick gitaway, and that their fingers never stutter when the guns begin to talk. She could not very well tell the children this is all hokum; they knew better, they had seen it with their own eyes. Had she nagged them about their viewing habits they would have branded her as an old nannygoat who probably doesn't even own a TV set and who wouldn't go to a tavern to look at one.

So she took their thirst for cowboy lore and used it against them. She compiled a reading list of books dealing with the West, and had her class writing book reviews at the drop of a sombrero. Soon they were telling her that real cowboys mend fences, nurse sick cattle, pitch hay. They were proud of themselves for discovering these things that the sponsors who make breakfast foods have never learned.

Here is a paragraph from *Scholastic Teacher* magazine: "For decades, drama critics and patrons have been bemoaning the fact that there is no 'national theatre' in America—an important cultural facet of any society which considers itself mature. Well, don't look now, but commercial TV has already that 'national theatre,' and right in the nation's living room. More and more English teachers who know a good thing when they see it are saying to their classes: Look now and we'll discuss the play in class Monday."

The article went on to tell how the best of the television dramas can be used by English teachers to increase in their students awareness and appreciation of literature. The article included a critique of *Cradle Song* to show how classroom discussion can be stimulated by such a play.

In one issue of *Scholastic Teacher,* William Sullivan, S.J., a teacher in Creighton University High School, explained how a teacher might use the telecast of Jean Anouilh's *The Lark* as a class assignment. He showed how a class could compare *The Lark,* a play about Joan of Arc, with two other plays that deal with the same subject—Shaw's *Saint Joan* and Maxwell Anderson's *Joan of Lorraine.* He suggested the plays might be compared with such biographies as V. Sackville-West's *Saint Joan of Arc* and Lucien Fabre's *Joan of Arc.*

Ted Cron, managing editor of the *Practical English* edition of *Scholastic Teacher* believes that teachers ought to do something for the worthwhile show and, through silence or other forms of non-indorsement, do something against the nuisance show. He has devised a plan that will do something for the worthwhile program and, for students and teachers as well.

He gets scripts of TV dramas that he feels will have value and prints them in the magazine in advance of telecast. He printed a scene from the television play, *Oliver Twist,* and along with it an excerpt from the novel on which the scene was based. He ran the script for *Shadow of a Soldier,* a play about the last days of General Grant's life, produced on *Our American Heritage* series.

These pre-printings give students and teacher time to stage the play in the classroom and to do some background reading before the professional production. One teacher wrote: "The lesson learned was evident the next day after we saw the TV performance. We learned that greater inflection in the voice makes for better delivery; that movement is part of acting in addition to just knowing lines. We knew where we had interpreted the author's meaning just right, and where we could have improved. We learned tricks of stage business that we shall remember for next time. . . . The entire experience was a thrilling one for the classes performing and a 'kick' for the rest of the school previewing."

Each week the *Practical English* edition of *Scholastic Teacher* devotes its back page to describing TV shows and radio programs that give promise for the week to come. Inside it reviews motion pictures and lists television shows that have been made available for classroom use. It informed teachers when kinescopes of Macbeth and Richard II, by *Hallmark Hall of Fame*, went on loan. It announced the release of several *Omnibus* films, among them the Constitution series and the Lincoln series. It announced when CBS made available for classroom use, *You Are There*, a series dramatizing historic incidents, and *The Search*, documentaries based on university experimentation.

Using television programs to add zest to classroom work will probably be done mostly on the grade-school and high-school level. However, there are times when things on television can be useful to a university teacher.

A professor who was teaching the philosophy of education to some graduate students found a program on NBC's *Outlook* valuable. He said the program ignited one of the most lively classroom discussions he had ever experienced. *Outlook* had asked two educators for two points of view on the purpose of education. The educators were Dr. William Carr, executive secretary of the National Education Association, and Dr. Robert Hutchins, former chancellor of the University of Chicago and now president of the Fund for the Republic.

Dr. Carr believes in education for everybody and in teaching things that are likely to be useful. Dr. Hutchins says that education for everybody is bound to be watery and that education's special province is to teach thought, not skills. Each man put forth his ideas exceedingly well. The ideas are of such stature that they are worthy of consideration at the university level.

As another instance of how a TV program could be used in a university class, let's look at NBC's *Comment*. In discussing the new American culture, Randall Jarrell, at that time consultant on poetry and English at the Library of Congress, took a dim view of things, but William Harlan Hale, editor of *Horizon*, was more optimistic.

Mr. Jarrell made his points by asking the audience a series of questions:

"Do you often read poetry for pleasure—Homer, or Milton, or Goethe, or Whitman, or Yeats?

"Do more of you know and own Frost's *Collected Poems* than know and own *Peyton Place?*

"Do you like things, people, animals, books, pictures for their own sakes, for what they really are like, rather than for the money or prestige you can get out of them?"

Mr. Hale, in defense of the new culture, said, "Thirty million copies of classical records are now sold annually. Many of them of obscure and difficult works. Obviously only a fraction of these go to the highbrows. A generation ago there were barely two dozen symphony orchestras in America; today there are far over 300, many of them amateur.

"Take books—a whole new industry of paperbacks has mushroomed since the war. We now see Plato and Aristotle printed in cheap editions of a hundred thousand or more.

"Take museums—attendance across the country last year was six times greater than the total crowds at major league baseball games."

Any teacher who has *Brave New World* on his reading list would have done well to ask his students to tune in Aldous Huxley's television appearance on ABC. Mr. Huxley wrote the novel twenty-five years ago. He painted a picture of a completely organized society in a way that will deeply disturb you if you have an ounce of individuality in your bones. During the intervening years, the whole world, especially Russia, has moved far enough in that direction so that Mr. Huxley can have the dubious satisfaction of saying I told you so.

On the television program Mr. Huxley explained that he believes the dictatorship of the future will be unlike any dictatorship of the past, and unlike the kind of dictatorship described in George Orwell's novel, *1984*. Orwell wrote about the old-fashioned type of dictator—like Stalin, Hitler and Mussolini—who ruled by force and fear. But the new dictatorship will rule not by force and fear but by lulling its subjects into loving their slavery. People will be happy in a situation in which they ought not be happy. In *Brave New World* this love of slavery was brought about largely through drugs and propaganda. Whenever anyone felt a little uneasy he popped a *soma* tablet into his mouth and presto all the world seemed bright and gay. Since *Brave New World* was written we have developed something known as happiness pills.

Propaganda in *Brave New World* started with the infants in the government rearing-centers. Beneath each little pillow was an earphone that played over and over some lesson that the child must grow up believing: "Alpha children wear grey. They work much harder than we do, because they're so frightfully clever. I'm really awfully glad I'm a Beta, because I don't work so hard. And then we are much better off than the Gammas and Deltas. Gammas are stupid. They all wear green, and Delta children wear khaki. Oh no, I don't want to play with Delta children . . ."

We already have a hint of this situation, Huxley thinks, in our radio and television commercials. Children go around chanting beer and toothpaste commercials. "We used to speak of the children of Europe as 'cannon fodder'; well, we are raising radio and television fodder. Trade journals tell us how necessary it is to get a hold on the children because then they will be loyal brand buyers later on. Can't you see that a political force could turn them into loyal ideology buyers when they grow up."

Subliminal projection, a new potential outlet for propaganda, is a subtlety that not even Mr. Huxley foresaw in *Brave New World*. The message is there and gone from the screen so fast that the eyes are not aware of it, but the mind is. Huxley fears that subliminal projection, television, happiness pills, atomic energy and other devices of our time will be used by wrong people for wrong means. These are all things that can be used to obtain power; the main defense against their misuse is the awareness of how they can be misused and finding ways of using them properly. It is the old story of eternal vigilance being the price of freedom.

It is easy to see that here are ideas that can help a teacher churn up a lively class discussion. But why bother with taking ideas from a television program when the same ideas are expressed in books?

A good teacher, artist that he is, realizes the value of change of pace; he realizes that taking ideas from a TV discussion can give them a here-and-nowness that a book might not give, at least to students who have been up to their ears in books for a long time.

A teacher of writing will sometimes take examples from such current things as a magazine article by John Hersey, a personal essay by E. B. White, or a newspaper column by Red Smith and not always depend on pieces that have long been embalmed between the covers of books. The fact that he can demonstrate principles of writing with pieces collected in a book is not the point; the point is that with the magazine article he might introduce a spirit of aliveness into the class and a realization that these principles are being used by professionals every day and are not just something old fuddy-duddies put into books for the confusion of young minds.

I confess I did some name-dropping in the past few pages. Intellectuals approve of such names as Robert Hutchins, Randall Jarrell and Aldous Huxley, and I am trying to assuage those intellectuals who get miffed when they hear the word television and education used in the same sentence.

Gilbert Seldes touched the heart of the matter when he said, in an article in *TV Guide,* that the intellectual is not really attacking television so much as he is defending his own interest which, by and large, is the empire of the printed page. He said that the highbrow can look at the screen and not really see what is going on there. "His training and his tradition and his prejudices prevent him from observing the actuality. He sees what he expects to see and what he expects to see is popular perversion of the whole culture that has come down to us through centuries of the printed word.

"What's happening to all of us is that we're going through a revolution. The prime communicator before the invention of printing was the preacher-orator; after that, print—the newspaper and the book and the magazine—took over. Now the power of print is being challenged. Power is shifting to the electronic medium, to the speaking image on the screen. Naturally, everyone who has spent years in the study of books, everyone who has written for print, everyone who has learned to respect whatever is between covers, feels resentful at the intrusion of the new force. I add myself to them and say, 'We have a vested interest in print and you, the managers of the electronic mass media, are lowering the value of our investment.'

"But as a citizen, I say that we who have had the great advantage of a book education owe it to the community to make terms with the new medium. If we are better educated than the average, we ought to be better able to *use* the mass media for the general good."

I can understand the intellectual's resentment of new gadgetry in communication because I resent the latter day gadgetry in transportation. In my heart I approve of only two methods of transportation—man's God-given legs and horseback. Yet I realize my favorites are not so efficient as the gasoline buggy and the flying machine. So I use the modern methods, but not without mingling animosity with appreciation, resentment with awe.

The intellectual will have to come to terms with television, uneasy though the terms may be. He may in time embrace television. It could happen. For years the movies nauseated him, but eventually he embraced them, renaming them the films and the cinema.

10. The Church and the Film Arts

THE DIMENSIONS OF MORALITY
A POSITIVE APPROACH

A HAPPY prospect as far as motion pictures and television are concerned is that the Catholic Church is showing an increasing interest in a positive program of appreciation. During the meeting of the International Catholic Film Office held in Havana, Pope Pius XII sent a message saying it is not enough for the Church to exert merely negative influence on films. He said, "This necessary action must be accomplished by educational endeavor in the strict sense." In a resolution, the International Catholic Film Office said that a critical sense in the cinema should be developed in schools, in seminaries, and in special groups formed for the purpose.

Why should the Catholic Church care whether or not anyone appreciates motion pictures or television shows? I suppose because it is interested in the arts no matter where they are found. The Church is interested in art, I would think, because it humanizes and refines the spirit and has a civilizing influence.

These are times ripe for a renewed interest in the arts, because the arts may help ease what thinking men see as a serious problem in this country—the problem of how to transcend affluence. For affluence not transcended is a downhill run to materialism. An over-supply of money and leisure lead to more gimmicks and gadgetry unless discernment puts them to better use.

THE DIMENSIONS OF MORALITY

Although the Church's first interest is in morality, it may consider art as morality's helpful ally. Art can serve as a partial shield against immorality. For instance, anyone sensitive to the art of the film could see *La Strada* or *Bachelor Party* without moral damage. Both pictures deal with immoral situations, but they do it in the right way. Instead of being morally damaging they are really morally uplifting. But someone blind to the art of the film might possibly see these pictures merely as things that titillate.

Some people do not think that sex is fit subject matter for fiction, and they do not see that art has anything to do with it. But it does. A story about a wife's unfaithfulness to her husband might be a dirty joke, and then again it might be Tolstoy's *Anna Karenina,* one of the great monuments of the human mind. The joke and *Anna Karenina* differ not in subject matter, but in their art—why the story is told and how it is told. Identical subject matter can be used to degrade the spirit or to uplift it.

If some modern writers took the subject matter of *Oedipus Rex* they would turn it into a sick, sick book. The play deals with incest, parricide, suicide and self-mutilation. Few gaudy drugstore novels can claim such an all-star lineup of evil. *Oedipus* is not a sick play but a great masterpiece because of the artistry of Sophocles.

I am not so naive as to think that Catholics will start showing discernment in motion pictures and television because Pope Pius XII said they should. No culture is ever advanced simply because someone says it ought to be. It is more complex and more mysterious than that. It flares as a spontaneous combustion of many inner smoulderings, hopes, dreams and urgings. Motion picture and television appreciation won't have a chance unless it finds itself in an atmosphere that is "right" for it, and this atmosphere is made up of many elements.

The atmosphere of Catholic culture is rapidly getting "right." I can document that statement in many ways just from my own observations, but I shall limit the documentation to three things—the growing interest of Catholic educators in art, the higher standards in the Catholic theater movement and the new introspection in the Catholic press.

A POSITIVE APPROACH

To start with an example close to the heart of this book—teachers in Catholic schools are becoming concerned about the "aesthetically squalid," a subject mentioned in the first chapter. To try to do something about it they have started cinema study clubs and are even discussing films in the classroom with all the respect that was, until recent years, reserved for the printed word. The teachers themselves are asking that someone help them develop better understanding of films and they are going to meetings held just for that purpose.

Speaking at one such meeting in Chicago in November, 1959, Father William Lynch, S.J., remarked that people sit in front of motion picture and television screens day after day trying to fill a frightening emptiness. Too often what they get from the screen is not filling, it lacks protein. When something of substance comes along many people avoid it fearing it will be uncomfortable to digest. They do not realize, said Father Lynch, that inside themselves they are craving the substantial. Inside every man there is a craving for closeness to things, to man, to God. In other words, there is a craving to get in touch with reality, and reality is substantial stuff, not fluff.

Father Lynch believes that it is the function of the motion picture, as it is the function of every art form, to uncover reality and not to cover it. Art can lead man bit by bit to a better understanding of things, himself and God. Art sharpens man's sensibilities, the whole range of human feelings that brings him in proper relationship with things, man and God.

Too often people seek things that cover reality, said Father Lynch, and they end up with films like *Samson and Delilah* and with fictional characters like Mike Hammer. The frightening thing is that once they start covering up reality in one field they will soon be covering it in other fields—they will cover up political, social and military realities as well.

In his book, *The Image Industries,* published in 1959, Father Lynch has as a recurrent theme a plea that the creative theologian and the artist get together because both have a desire in common—the true interpretation of man. Each wishes to say in his own way that man is a great and complicated and fascinating being whether for good or for bad. The trouble is that they do not often see the bond of sympathy that unites them.

Up until now, Father Lynch says, it has been the moralist, the censor and the moral theologian who have policed the artist. The artist resented their interference because he felt they did not understand art. However, the creative theologian can find rapport with the artist because they are both enemies of bad workmanship and both rejoice in a work of art when they meet it.

Why have the theologian and the artist failed to find rapport? Why has the aesthetically squalid cheapened so many spirits? Why are people afraid to seek reality in the arts? Why do so many avoid the search and the honest adventure that the arts encourage and instead seek refuge in security and softness?

Philip Scharper, who spoke at the same meeting as did Father Lynch, puts part of the blame on education. He says that for too many years education has treated the arts as though they were second-rate subjects. If through the years poetry had not been so poorly taught, and if through the years drama had not been so ineptly taught and tastelessly produced, motion picture audiences might be better able to accept a film of substance. An abuse of an art, like any other abuse, ultimately exacts a revenge.

If motion pictures miraculously matured over night, would the people we have educated be mature enough to accept them? Mr. Scharper wonders if perhaps they would not sigh for the sentimentality and the tin-whistle cheerfulness that they have come to depend on to keep them from facing reality.

What Mr. Scharper says about art having had second-class treatment in the schools is true. But it is rapidly ceasing to be true. The fact that so many teachers gathered to hear what he and Father Lynch had to say is some indication of a growing interest and concern about the state of the arts.

It was especially heartening to find this concern reflected at a national meeting of the Catholic Theatre Conference. Less than a generation ago the theatre at Catholic University stood on a somewhat lonely eminence. The Catholic Theatre Conference seems to have as its basic tenet *the higher the standards of art the more successfully truth is served.* It stresses that a shoddy production is dishonest to those who view it and a waste of time and talent for those who present it. Its recurrent theme is that students should be taught to distinguish the best from the second best and that taste ought to be taught as well as morality.

The exhibits at a Catholic Theatre Conference national meeting proved that these principles are acted on. Photographs of plays that some high schools and colleges had presented showed that Catholic theatre standards had climbed since the organization's founding a quarter century ago. The choice of plays and the sets and costumes are far superior to what they were a generation ago.

As a nun explained to me at one of the meetings, "Catholic Theater Conference has broadened our understanding of what a religious play is. We used to think it was about a priest or a nun, or one in which a girl leaves for the convent as the final curtain falls. Now we know that a play is religious if it presents evil as evil and good as good."

Another favorable sign is the growing interest of the Catholic press in culture. Here are condensations from speeches given at a Catholic Press Association convention:

• The Catholic press should do more about the arts—painting, sculpture, music, architecture, drama. There is not enough effort being made to educate and refine the taste. A genuine Catholic culture does not just worry about labor relations, it is also concerned with the liberal and the fine arts.

• Humor is something the Catholic press could use more of. The Catholic mind has always known the saving grace of laughter. It is not fitting for the Catholic press to wear such a solemn face.

• The Catholic book critic must be careful not to confuse the creative artist with the sly pornographer. The artist deals with evil because it is a part of life, but he shows evil as evil; the pornographer deals with evil because he finds it saleable, and he makes evil seem good.

• The Catholic critic sees so many harmful books that he often resorts to sigh-of-relief reviewing. He praises a pallid book because it will do nobody any harm—it will do nobody any good, either. This leads to sigh-of-relief award-giving. Awards sometimes go to pallid books simply because such books are harmless.

• Catholic publications ought to aim at being as technically perfect as secular publications. Editors need to remember that being in favor of virtue does not save one from being a bad artist or a bad critic.

I present these fragments to document my opinion that the Church's interest in developing discrimination in films and in TV has a chance of fulfillment. The times are right. Mature attitudes in Catholic education and in the Catholic press help create an atmosphere in which all arts have a chance to flourish.

Fortunately, the Church realizes that the best thing to do about the aesthetically squalid is not to keep complaining about it; that only calls attention to it and often promotes it. The best thing is to implant some attitudes that will help the public see the aesthetically squalid for what it is.

Some Catholics will not approve of this system, not because they are Catholics but because they are people with a certain cast of mind. The world is shot through with people who have no patience with the positive. They have no patience with the long, slow educative process that attempts to lead rather than to drive. They get their satisfaction from legislation, not education. They are more attracted to the don'ts of life than to the do's. They enjoy a bunch of rules and regulations with which they can club others over the head.

Postscript

BEFORE starting this book you were probably your own favorite motion picture and television critic. Chances are you still are. This is all right as long as you make yourself worthy of the title. To be worthy of the title you need standards beyond, "It was good, I liked it." You need enough feeling for the medium not to complain that "It wasn't like the book." And your interest in the picture ought to go beyond. "Who's playing in it?" You ought to be wary of letting the subject matter prejudice you in favor of a picture or against it, realizing that the question is, *how* was the subject matter handled?

As your own favorite critic you ought to be discerning enough to realize that the motion picture and the television industries are not responsible for *all* the moral problems that grow out of them. Anyone who caters to the worthless in films and TV shows is encouraging somebody to litter God's world with ugliness, and that is a moral problem. Anyone who caters to the worthless is killing time, chipping off chunks of his life, a modified form of suicide and that can be a moral problem, too.

My hope is that this book will help you avoid some of the worthless things in films and on TV. As I said in the opening sentence, too often I hear the lean mice of trivialities nibbling at my allotted chunk of time. I am sorry to say that neither this book, nor cinema study clubs, nor anything else will drive the lean mice completely from your life. It is a part of your destiny, as it is every man's, to keep setting traps for them, knowing the while that you will never catch them all. The very next time you are staring at a screen you may hear a scurry in the dusky corner of conscience. And you will know that trivialities are still around.

Appendices

Forming a Film Study Group

CINEMA study clubs are sprouting all over the country. Sometimes I get a letter asking for advice on how to start one. To anyone contemplating a cinema club I offer six suggestions:

1. Find a good teacher.

Some people might hesitate to wire a house or perform an appendectomy without some training and yet not hesitate to hack away at a work of art despite a lack of background. That is why a club needs a teacher who knows film standards; otherwise well-intentioned people who know nothing about films might band together merely to applaud what is mediocre and never get around to developing good critical judgments.

2. Read the critical reviews.

People are more apt to check motion pictures than television programs in advance. Motion pictures cost money and some people put more value on money than on time and so are prompted to do a little investigating for that reason if for no other. Still, a good number buy tickets blindly. I will always remember that during the opening sequence of *North by Northwest* a man sitting next to me said to his wife, "We saw this before. Might as well leave. If we had looked we'd a known."

From a cross-section of critical writing you might check reviews in *The Saturday Review, The New Republic, Variety,*

Film Quarterly, Sight and Sound, Films in Review, The New Statesman, The New York *Times*, The New York *Herald Tribune, Time, Newsweek, Commonweal, Our Sunday Visitor*, and *Jubilee*.

A useful weekly publication is *Filmfacts;* it devotes all of its space to digests of reviews of current pictures. Another, *The Green Sheet*, is published monthly by the Film Estimates Board of National Organizations.

Sometimes a critic will mislead you—especially if you misread him—but in the long run a good critic is more of a service than a disservice. He can help your attitudes, tastes and judgments change for the best. And they should change, because growth means changing in the right direction.

You must have noticed that some of the films you once enjoyed no longer have any appeal for you. Perhaps you sat up late to watch an old film on television, something you remembered as wonderful twenty years ago; but now as you watch it with more maturity you realize it is empty. It is natural for you to grow away from some things.

On rare occasions it works the other way around. Not long ago I saw *Citizen Kane* and realized for the first time why it is an outstanding motion picture. When I had seen it twenty years ago I had found it an interesting story, but not much beyond that. In the intervening years I have learned something about how to look at motion pictures.

A critic is more to be pitied than scorned. His job is filled with occupational hazards, not the least of which can be the death of awe and wonder inside himself. Often he finds that what is sold as recreation lacks the power to re-create, and so he completes his appointed rounds feeling enervated and dull, as though someone had slammed a broad, flat board across his spirit. He worries about his taste buds hardening and sometimes he shuns the motion picture and television screens for a time hoping that his taste buds will regain sensitivity if the calluses peel off.

Serious films often leave him aching for the easement that comes with the purging of emotions during a tragedy well done. So many foreign films cause this; they make life seem lackluster and the world washed-thin.

Now that foreign films have come up allow me to detour for a few paragraphs to talk about them. You must have noticed that when several people talk seriously about motion pictures someone is almost certain to say, "Why can't Hollywood make pictures like the foreign films?" At such times I count to ten before answering.

Hollywood turns out some drivel, but the foreign films can out-drivel Hollywood. The tendency is to recall *Great Expectations, Brief Encounter* and *Henry V,* and to forget the drivel.

The foreign film deserved its place in the sun right after World War II. Only a few dozen pictures were sent over each year and they were the pick of the crop. Besides, foreign producers seemed to be doing more sincere work then; they did not have much money and their equipment left much to be desired. But when foreign films started flooding us it was clear that there are far more mediocrities among them than among American films. Hollywood turns out a higher percentage of films of merit.

Not long ago I saw an Italian film as part of a film series that is supposed to offer the best of foreign pictures. Maybe the members of the committee who booked this picture thought it was artistic because the actors spoke in Italian. Had Hollywood filmed the same script they would have come out saying, "What a horror!"

Soon after that I saw a French film that made me think all the way through that I had come in somewhere in the middle. The story line was blurred and the characters were unbelievable. It was badly put together, as though a group of untalented amateurs had tried their hands at film-making. This is the kind of criticism that can rarely be leveled at Hollywood; even at its worst, Hollywood is usually professional.

People enamored of foreign movies may have sat through that French film feeling they were seeing Great Art unfold before their eyes. Again, maybe because the dialogue is in a foreign tongue. Maybe when they read such lines at the bottom of the screen as, "You were just a flea and I taught you how to live," and "You win a woman the way you win a war," they feel they are touching the hem of genius.

Again the admonition: use the critics. Some foreign films in the past few years were worth the trans-Atlantic shipping costs and the critics would have led you to them—*La Strada, The Green Man, Black Orpheus, 400 Blows, Wild Strawberries, Ikiru, The Seventh Seal, The Cranes are Flying.*

Let the critic sift out the great drifts of mediocrity for you. His job is to sift, and sift, and sift through the gray dust so that every so often he might shout and hold up a bright and shining object. Don't you bother doing all that sifting. Just listen for the shout and then run toward the bright and shining object.

3. Look at films that are worth your time.

In the back of this book there is a list of film distributors. You can get catalogues from them, but not every film in every catalogue will be worth your time. So the question is, what films to rent?

TV Movie Almanac, published in paperback by Bantam Books, will help you decide what pictures are worth sitting through. It gives a capsule review of 5,000 films and rates them: four stars, excellent; three stars, good; two stars, fair; and one star, poor. Of the 5,000 films rated, the almanac gives four stars to 179 of them.

I remember with four-star pleasure many of the films listed in the almanac as four-star: *Body and Soul, Boomerang, Brief Encounter, Citizen Kane, Encore, The Fallen Idol, The Fugitive, Great Expectations, Green Pastures, Hamlet, High Noon,*

La Strada, Ox Bow Incident, Quiet Man, Red River, The River, Stagecoach, The Third Man, Tight Little Island, The Time of Your Life, Treasure of the Sierra Madre. A cinema study club looking for something to show could do worse than to use that brief list of films.

Another book every cinema club ought to own is Arthur Knight's, *The Liveliest Art,* a lively history of motion pictures. It was published by Macmillan in 1957 and has since been issued in paperback in the New American Library series. In it there is an index to films discussed in the book with information about where each film may be rented.

I asked Mr. Knight for a list of films that would make a good introductory series for a study club. The showman in him won out briefly over the historian when he said that he would get the series off to a lively start with a good musical comedy, such as *Singin' in the Rain.* But from that point on his list is chronological and very much an historical study.

Mr. Knight said that there ought to be a film by David Wark Griffith, the father of film technique. Griffith perceived that a movie should not be a stage play committed to celluloid. He made the camera move around—in close, far back, up high, down low—always searching for the most telling position. Although he did not originate camera movement, he was the first to use it for aesthetic reasons and not merely to show movement for the sake of movement. He also realized how the emotions can be influenced by putting one scene in juxtaposition with another, and so he brought artistry to the cutting bench. *Birth of a Nation* would be a good Griffith film to show.

For the next picture in the series, Mr. Knight suggests one from the Golden Era of the German film, perhaps *The Last Laugh* or *Variety.* The Golden Era lasted but a short time, roughly through the early years of the 1920's. The Germans refined the grammar of the film developed by Griffith and developed a new subtlety of acting that still seems right for the screen. They explored new and exciting ways of staging and found new ways of using the camera as an artistic instrument rather than as merely a recording instrument. They were fascinated by the camera on wheels and had it rolling restlessly about to bring a fluidity to the screen that it had not known until that time.

Next on the series might well come a film from the experimental period in Russia—*Potemkin* or *Ten Days That Shook the World*. In the late 1920's, Sergei Eisenstein conducted some exciting experiments in editing. He took Griffith's idea of getting an emotional effect by splicing scenes in juxtaposition and tried to find new artistic possibilities in it.

Mr. Knight's list then brings the study club back to the United States for one of the great comedies of the late silent era. He suggests a Charlie Chaplin, or Buster Keaton, or Harold Lloyd picture. To close the silent era, Mr. Knight believes there is no better picture to show than the French *Passion of Joan of Arc*. He feels that this picture best summarizes and characterizes the entire era of production in the twenties.

The film, *The Coming of Sound*, would fit well into the series at this point. In it are excerpts from *The Jazz Singer*, the picture that introduced sound, and *The Lights of New York*, the first full-length, all-talking picture, a Disney sound cartoon and a Robert Benchley short. This picture can be rented from the Museum of Modern Art Film Library.

Film-makers became so fascinated by sound that they almost forgot that a motion picture should be seen more than heard. The public began to speak of the talkies rather than the movies, for pictures were talking a great deal more than they were moving. Perhaps it was the Frenchman René Clair who discovered how to use sound intelligently. Mr. Knight feels that a René Clair picture ought to be shown at this stage in the series, and suggests *Sous les Toits de Paris*.

Mr. Knight says that screen writers had to learn what to say and what to leave unsaid, and feels that Dudley Nichols, the writer, and John Ford, the director, gave us one of the best early examples of how sight and sound ought to work together. That is why *The Informer* is scheduled for this part of the series. Next comes Orson Welles' *Citizen Kane*. It makes the list because it is experimental in the extreme—in photography, lighting, sets, music.

Somewhere along about here the club ought to have an evening or two of documentaries. Mr. Knight suggests *The City, The River, Desert Victory, Man of Aran, Listen to Britain*.

To close the series, Mr. Knight suggests some foreign films: *The Seventh Seal* (Swedish); *Brief Encounter* (British); *Rashomon* (Japanese); *Open City* or *Bicycle Thief* (Italian).

The historical approach is one way to film appreciation. A dimension is added to understanding when you know what has preceded it. If a club starts out across the historical route, it needs a teacher to explain why each film has been chosen and to help the audience see each picture through the eyes of the audience it was made for.

Film appreciation can be advanced through other approaches, say through a series of post-World War II pictures. It is possible to appreciate the films of John Ford, David Lean and Akira Kurosawa without knowing where those directors fit into film history, just as it is possible to admire the work of Rouault, Maillol and Gropius without knowing art history.

Let me warn that just seeing films will not necessarily lead to discernment. I know a woman who saw a motion picture every afternoon for years and never got beyond, "It was good, I liked it," or "It was no good, I didn't like it." If exposure alone turned the trick, ushers in movie houses would be distinguished critics and guards in art museums would be connoisseurs. Contact helps, but contact with guidance is what really helps.

4. Read some books about motion pictures.

Next to a good teacher and some good critics, books are helpful guides. Books alone are not enough. As Clifton Fadiman said, to be a sucessful parent it is not enough to read a book titled *How to Be a Good Parent.* A good parent is a person who is good, kind and wise, and books won't turn the trick. In the same way, the recognition of what is good in motion pictures and television grows from a cultivated milieu and not from reading. But books might save a study club from discussing films in glittering generalities while still ignorant of the more mundane problems of technique. Books can help anchor observations; otherwise the club's discussions might go into orbit and just revolve in outer space.

On page 184 is a list of books a study club might find useful.

5. Follow screen credits.

When Jessamyn West was told that William Wyler wanted to direct a film adaptation of her book, *The Friendly Persuasion,* she asked, "Who is William Wyler?" When asked if she had ever seen *Mrs. Miniver,* or *The Best Years of Our Lives,* or *Wuthering Heights,* or *Little Foxes,* or *Roman Holiday,* she answered that she had seen all of them, and liked them. William Wyler, she was told, had made all of them.

Miss West, who had long been annoyed by people who enjoy books but do not bother to notice the name of the author, understood how crass her question was. People who know something about motion pictures follow the names of the directors as closely as people who know fiction follow the names of novelists.

People who know little about films are only interested in the names of actors and actresses. When the credits are crawling across the screen they use those moments to make last-minute comments to their neighbor.

To give the film club members a start, here are the names of a few directors worth following: John Ford, John Huston, Vincente Minnelli, Elia Kazan, Delbert Mann, George Stevens, Fred Zinnemann, William Wyler, Alfred Hitchcock, Carol Reed, David Lean, Ingmar Bergman, Akira Kurosawa, Frederico Fellini, Vittorio DeSica, René Clair, Jean Renoir.

6. Try your hand at writing reviews.

Each member of the club ought to express his thoughts on each film in about a 300-word written review. There is nothing like writing to develop mental discipline and definite critical observation. Writing discourages half-thoughts and half-opinions.

In the beginning everyone will find it difficult to review a picture having seen it but once. That will be especially true if the club is studying film technique; such a study sensitizes everyone to so many things that it is frustrating to try to grab everything at once.

Someone in the club should compile reviews that were written about the film under discussion at the time of its release. This will make it possible for the club members to compare their observations with those of the professionals. No one should expect, of course, to agree with the professionals in every instance; they do not always agree with each other.

It is not important that you try to prove you are right and the professional is wrong. The important thing is to try to realize when you are wrong. I must face up to being wrong every time I come across laudatory things written about Charles Chaplin. He has more genius than meets my eye. He has always been one of my blind spots. But I know that I am not right and all the other critics wrong. I am not going to act as if I enjoy Chaplin when I don't. That is important: never fake enjoyment just to be on the side of the initiated.

One advantage of writing reviews is that it may lead some hesitant members into making observations that are worth making. The biggest advantage of all is that the written word may have a quieting effect on members who join a discussion group because it provides them with a ready audience.

Questions for Film Study

THE following questions may be helpful to film study groups:

1. Is this an original screenplay, or an adaptation from a novel, a short story, a stage play, or a teledrama?

2. Name the director, the producer, the writer.

3. What is the theme?

4. Is the story line so simple that you could tell it in a few sentences, or is it so complex that the writer is trying to say too many things in his allotted amount of screen time?

5. Is the film so unified that nothing can be added to it or subtracted from it without doing it harm?

6. Does the beginning get attention in the *right* way, or is it out of key with the rest of the picture?

7. As for the sub-plot, does it loom too large? Is it so woven into the main plot that it enriches the main plot and advances it?

8. Does the conflict build to an inevitable climax? Does the climax resolve the conflict effectively?

9. Does the ending have a feeling of ending about it: that this is a good place to get off?

10. If the film is non-fiction are the facts presented in large blocks of material, like-things grouped with like-things? What is the framework on which these facts are hung?

11. Was the tempo in editing exaggerated at any place for an emotional effect?

12. Are scenes ever placed in juxtaposition to give an emotional effect?

13. Are there any clichés in dialogue, in characters, in props, in situations?

14. Are the characters creatures of flesh and blood drawn in the round with faults, impulses, hopes and fears like ourselves?

15. Are there any inconsistencies in the actions of the characters?

16. Are minor characters as believable and as real as the main characters?

17. How are visual symbols and outward signs used to tell of a character's emotions and attitudes?

18. Does the dialogue have the ring of conversation?

19. Were there any interesting bits of "stage business"?

20. Do the sets and the costumes and the makeup all help in telling something about the characters?

21. Does the film lean toward realism or toward romanticism?

22. Is the style of acting suitable to the type of story being told?

23. Are actors and actresses properly cast? Did all roles need professionals or could some of them have been played by people in the walk of life depicted in the story?

24. If the sound system broke would you still be able to follow most of the story through the action on the screen? Is the picture too talky? Are there places where action might be substituted for dialogue?

25. Which sequence depends most on "build-up" for its effectiveness?

26. Does the narrator say only what he needs to say, or does he talk too much? What about his delivery: does it have the good taste that comes with proper dignity of spirit, or is it too cute or too pompous?

27. In adapting the story from a novel or a stage play were many changes made? Were those changes necessary? Should others have been made?

28. Is the music functional?

29. Are sound effects ever exaggerated to give an emotional effect?

30. Is color used for an emotional effect? Does this story lend itself to black and white or to color?

31. Are such strong emotions as grief and joy well handled or were they at times lacking in restraint? Did sentiment ever slop over into sentimentality?

32. Does the audience learn of acts of violence through what Henry James called "strong specification"?

33. Are there any instances of a director writing an editorial with his camera through the way he composes his shot?

34. Is movement ever speeded up or slowed down for an effect? Is there any instance in which a director prolonged time in a sequence, or shortened it, for a psychological effect?

35. Can you sense artistic truth in this picture? Does it have in it the texture of life, what Henry James called "felt life"? Does it help you live beyond what your own living can be? Does it make you "see" more and understand more and feel more deeply so that you better realize some aspect of life if only momentarily? Does it bring an aesthetic experience to the point that the senses are heightened and sharpened?

36. Does this picture tend to refine the spirit or to coarsen it? If a tragedy, does it give easement to the spirit by purging the emotions or does it leave you edgy with unreleased feeling? If a comedy, does it spring from an imagination that has freshness and refinement or from one that is gross and fumbling? Is the humor slapstick, or of a more civilized kind; that which laughs when it sees a sense of values go askew?

37. Does the picture try to propagandize?

38. Does the picture tell honestly about a culture, a way of life, a set of values, other than our own?

39. Does the story seem not only possible but probable; in other words, does it lead the audience to a willing suspension of disbelief?

40. Did the writer use coincidence just to make things easy for himself?

41. Is there any tactility in the film: does it make you "feel" anything in the mind—wetness, cold, heat?

42. Is the subject matter such that it might prejudice you in favor of or prejudice you against the picture?

43. Does the title of the picture mislead? Were the newspaper ads misleading? Were the scenes selected for preview purposes misleading?

44. If you were rating this picture on a four-star system, how many stars would you give it? Was it worth your time? Would you care to sit through it again? Would you need to see it more than once to write an adequate review?

45. Do you expect that you might think more highly of this picture ten years from now? Would you have thought better of it a few years ago?

Some Sources for 16mm Films

Athena Films
570 Seventh Avenue
New York 36, New York

Brandon Films
200 West 57th Street
New York 19, New York

British Information Services
and Contemporary Films
267 West 25th Street
New York 1, New York

Cinema 16
175 Lexington Avenue
New York 16, New York

Contemporary Films
267 West 25th Street
New York 1, New York

Encyclopaedia Films
1150 Wilmette Avenue
Wilmette, Illinois

Film Images
1860 Broadway
New York 23, New York

Ideal Pictures
58 South Water Street
Chicago, Illinois

International Film Bureau
57 East Jackson Boulevard
Chicago 4, Illinois

Museum of Modern Art Film Library
11 West 53rd Street
New York 19, New York

Pictura Films
41 Union Square, West
New York 3, New York

Trans-World Films, Incorporated
53 West Jackson Boulevard
Chicago 4, Illinois

United World Films
1445 Park Avenue
New York 29, New York

Bibliography

HERE are some books worth the attention of anyone who wants to develop some capacity for motion picture criticism.

The Liveliest Art by Arthur Knight (Macmillan, 1957; paperback, New American Library, 1959)

Case History of a Movie by Dore Schary (Random House, 1950)

Picture by Lillian Ross (Rinehart, 1952)

To See the Dream by Jessamyn West (Harcourt, Brace, 1957)

Screen Playwriting by Lewis Herman (World, 1952)

The World of Robert Flaherty by Richard Griffith (Duell, Sloan and Pearce, 1953)

The Image Industries by William F. Lynch, S.J. (Sheed & Ward, 1959)

Criticism and Censorship by Walter Kerr (Bruce, 1954)

How to Shoot a Movie Story by David A. Englander and Arthur L. Gaskill (Morgan & Morgan, 1959)

Film as Art by Rudolf Arnheim (University of California Press, 1957)

The Art of the Film by Ernest Lindgren (Allen & Unwin, 1948)

The Lion's Share by Bosley Crowther (Dutton, 1957)

Documentary and Experimental Films (Museum of Modern Art Film Library, 1959)